Healthy Indian Cooking for Diabetes

Azmina Govindji RD & Sanjeev Kapoor

Healthy Indian Cooking for Diabetes

Delicious Khana for Life

Azmina Govindji RD & Sanjeev Kapoor

Diabetes UK

Kyle Cathie Limited

Acknowledgements

Many people have been involved in the publication of this book; it's not just about the authors. I would like to thank my professional dietetic colleagues, Smita Ganatra RD, Sema Jethwa RD and Chetali Agrawal RD for their expertise and research. Thanks also go to the diligent Dr Wendy Doyle RD for meticulously analysing the recipes.

Many sources have helped me to devise the information in this book and I would like to acknowledge them here: *The Composition and Nutrient Content of Foods Commonly Consumed by South Asians in the UK* by Patricia A. Judd, Tashmin Kassam-Khamis and Jane E. Thomas (published by the Aga Khan Health Board for the UK); McCance and Widdowson's *The Composition of Foods* (published by The Food Standards Agency); *Food Portion Sizes* (published by The Food Standards Agency); and *The Calorie Carb and Fat Bible* (published by Weight Loss Resources UK).

I would also like to thank the Nutrition and Dietetic Services of Leicester Royal Infirmary, for allowing me to use the plate model (on page 18) from their site: www.leicestershire-diabetes.org.uk.

And not forgetting my mother and sister for inspiring me to enjoy Indian cuisine.

And last but certainly not least, I would like to thank the collaborators of this publication – Diabetes UK for yet again having the confidence in me to write another book with them, my charismatic co-author, Sanjeev, for taking on all my recommendations with grace, and of course my editors Muna Reyal and Sophie Allen, who always work with great patience and professionalism.

Azmina Govindji

I have authored many books but *Healthy Indian Cooking for Diabetes* with Azmina has been a great learning experience. Thanks to her for taking on the idea and making it happen so brilliantly!

I wish to acknowledge my content team led by Rajeev who has been thoroughly involved in all the coordination activities of the book. All through the process ideas from Harpal and Neena have helped us along.

I want to mention Anupa, Afsheen, Trupti, Saurabh, Mohsin and Suryakant for doing the trials and retrials with a smile. They have exhibited super efficiency in spite of the pressure put on them. Thanks to Tripta for editorial support and meeting all the deadlines.

I also take this opportunity to thank the one lovely person who has successfully ingrained in my family the habit of eating healthily and low fat, my wife Alyona.

Sanjeev Kapoor

NOTES:

All dishes serve four, unless otherwise stated.
When 'spray oil' is mentioned, please use no more than ½ tablespoon of oil.
When garlic or root ginger is described as 'minced', this means mash/grind it until it becomes a paste.
The nutritional analysis at the end of each recipes is for one person.

contents

a word from Sanjeev

Diabetes is a complex condition and has been associated with diet for centuries. In fact, the science of nutrition has greater application in diabetes than in many other clinical conditions.

Healthy Indian Cooking for Diabetes will help you control your blood glucose levels through diet. I must add that, along with eating healthily, being more physically active is also important.

It is known that the South Asian people from the Indian sub-continent are more likely than other races to develop Type 2 diabetes. But this need not be a deterrent to enjoying a full life. And, most important, you don't have to give up Indian food, for it can be altered to suit your condition without sacrificing the taste.

Food is a great healer. There is not only sustenance in it but also a lot of comfort. If there is good, healthy food on the table for you half the battle is won! My collection of recipes aims at adapting daily Indian recipes, making them healthier and more balanced. The recipes will guide you through the simple steps of cooking. The variety, hand-picked from different regions of beautiful India, will regale you meal after meal.

And as we all understand that a healthy meal goes a long way, I have presented recipes for all courses including desserts. Yes, indeed, people with diabetes can indulge their sweet tooth occasionally! All the recipes serve four people, keeping in mind that each dish forms part of a menu consisting of several complementary dishes.

I hope you enjoy this authentic Indian food, full of flavour and goodness.

Sanjeev Kapoor

foreword by Diabetes UK

Balancing your diet when you are diagnosed with diabetes can be challenging.

The food choices you make and your eating habits are very important in helping you manage your diabetes, but this should not stop you being able to enjoy a wide variety of foods as part of a balanced, healthy diet.

Healthy Indian Cooking for Diabetes is a great tool in your quest to find that balance, while still allowing you to eat the foods you love. Full of handy tips and delicious recipes, *Healthy Indian Cooking for Diabetes* shows you how you can maintain a healthy weight without compromising on taste.

If you don't have diabetes, managing your weight and leading a healthy lifestyle can actually delay or prevent the onset of Type 2 diabetes. The recipes in this book are not just for people with diabetes, but for everybody who enjoys Indian food and wants to stick to a healthy weight.

We hope you enjoy using them.

Douglas Smallwood
Chief Executive
Diabetes UK

Diabetes
UK

The charity for
people with diabetes
Registered charity no. 215199

diabetes – the facts

So, you've been diagnosed with diabetes? You may have had the condition for some time, or perhaps you've just found out and are anxious about the future. Whatever your circumstances, you should know that the way you feel about having diabetes – such as 'Why me?', or 'What will my family and community think?' – will influence how you deal with the situation. With the right attitude and knowledge, you can enjoy a full life with confidence. And if you care for someone who has diabetes, you can positively influence their health by being supportive and informed. Congratulations on taking the first step by picking up this book.

Healthy Indian Cooking for Diabetes will be your treasure chest of tools that will give you practical hints and tips on how to live healthily with your diabetes, as well as sumptuous recipes that the whole family can enjoy. Be assured that the information is in line with recommen-dations for people with diabetes, based on solid scientific facts. We don't offer you anything that hasn't been fully researched, and our guidelines will help you make sense of the science.

Trying to make friends with your condition is a mind-blowing thought, but it is a good first step. As with many difficult situations in life, the experience can often provide you with an important lesson. And that lesson may be that if you take the time to care for yourself, you will be more able to care for other important people in your life.

Just being South Asian puts you at risk…

Is it true that diabetes is more common in South Asian people from the Indian sub-continent? Just look around you. There's very likely to be someone in your family who has diabetes, and certainly many people in your community. Three hundred people are diagnosed with diabetes every day in the UK, of which 60 are from the South Asian community. We are just genetically more predisposed to Type 2 diabetes.

Let's put this fact into some sort of perspective. If you are white and over 40 years old, and you have one or more of the risk factors of diabetes – for example, a family member has diabetes; you're overweight or have a high waist measurement; or you have high blood pressure or heart disease – you are at increased risk of developing Type 2 diabetes. But if you're South Asian with one or more of these risk factors, you only need to be 25 years old to have this increased risk.

There are high rates of untreated diabetes, abnormal cholesterol levels and high blood pressure among South Asians in the UK. The good news is that if you watch what you eat and your lifestyle habits, you could prevent or delay the onset of these conditions. You are also more prone to developing heart disease if you have diabetes, but if you manage your diabetes well, you can significantly reduce your risks.

Watch your waist

How much you weigh is a useful indication as to your long-term health, but an increasing amount of research is indicating the importance of where your fat is distributed rather than simply how heavy you are. Carrying excess weight around the waist (known as central obesity, or being apple-shaped) is a leading risk factor for heart disease, high blood pressure and Type 2 diabetes.

As a race, South Asians are more likely than the general population to carry too much weight around the middle.

Measuring your waist is an easy way to establish whether you are an 'apple' shape (having more weight on your waist than on your hips) or 'pear' shape (with more weight on your hips than on your waist). To do this, find a tape measure and then locate the spot midway between the bottom of your ribs and the top of your hips; you may find it easier to measure just above your belly button. Take the measurement after breathing out.

The chart below will help you establish how you shape up. To put it simply, if you have a risky waist measurement, you must take action now.

Waist measurement for:	At increased risk
South Asian men	90cm (35 inches)
South Asian women	80cm (31.5 inches)

What is diabetes?

When you have diabetes, the amount of glucose (sugar) in your blood is abnormally high. This is because your body isn't able to use the glucose properly. Insulin, a hormone produced in the pancreas (a gland situated next to the stomach), is needed to help the glucose move from the blood either into your muscles, where you can use it for energy straight away, or into your liver, where you can store it for use later. If there is not enough insulin, or if the insulin you have does not work properly, glucose can build up in your blood.

If you have Type 1 diabetes, this means that you are severely lacking in insulin and must be treated by injections of insulin, as well as eating a healthy diet.

If you have Type 2 diabetes (which is much more common than Type 1), you are not dependent on insulin injections since your body is still able to produce some insulin, but simply not as much as it needs. In 80 per cent of cases people who have Type 2 diabetes are overweight. This type of diabetes can be treated by a healthy diet and regular physical activity, or in combination with tablets or insulin injections. It is this type of diabetes that is the focus of this book.

Understanding your blood glucose levels

If you choose to eat foods that make your blood glucose (or sugar) level go up quickly, this encourages insulin levels in your body to rise swiftly. The more you do this, the more your body gets used to high circulating levels of insulin, and, in time, you can become resistant to the effect of your own insulin, especially if you are overweight. So you are in effect insulin resistant. Research has shown that putting on weight around the middle is linked with this 'insulin resistance' (IR). And

insulin resistance is linked with Type 2 diabetes, as well as cardiovascular disease and metabolic syndrome. The latter, also known as Syndrome X or insulin resistance syndrome, can be a precursor to Type 2 diabetes.

For those with diabetes, maintaining blood glucose levels within a healthy range – avoiding 'highs' and 'lows' – is the essential aim of treatment. And the means to controlling your blood glucose levels is by leading a healthy lifestyle. In return for the initial effort required to change your lifestyle you will be protecting yourself against the long-term damage people with diabetes can suffer to their heart, kidneys, eyes and nerves.

Low blood glucose

The medical term for having low blood glucose is hypoglycaemia or 'hypo'. Hypos are generally most likely to occur in people treated with insulin or certain tablets. Ask your healthcare team about this. It can be caused by:

- A delayed or missed meal or snack
- Doing more strenuous activity than usual
- Taking too much medication for diabetes
- Drinking alcohol on an empty stomach

Sometimes there may be no obvious explanation. Signs and symptoms of a hypo vary from person to person, but the common ones are light-headedness, feeling faint, sweating, shaking, hunger and confusion. Treat a hypo immediately by taking three or more glucose tablets or a sugary drink to raise your blood glucose quickly. Then, within half an hour, take something more substantial, such as a glass of milk and a slice of granary toast, to maintain a good blood glucose level.

food – the facts

Now you know the significance of your blood glucose levels in relation to your diabetes, and the importance of maintaining them at a healthy level, it is plain to see that what you eat is the most important part of your diabetes treatment. Insulin or tablets are not a substitute for a good diet. Whether you need to take medication or not, what you eat and how much and how often you eat have a significant effect on the amount of glucose, and also of fat (like cholesterol), in your blood.

Quick tip: Choose foods that help to stabilise your blood glucose levels, and avoid putting on weight around your middle.

For people with diabetes, what happens when you eat carbohydrates, or 'carbs' as they are often known, is really important. These are starchy foods such as potatoes, rice, bread and roti/chapatis, and sugary foods such as cakes, mithai and biscuits. Carbohydrates are digested in the gut and broken down into tiny particles, which are actually glucose molecules. These molecules move through your gut wall into the blood and this makes your blood glucose levels go up. To summarise:

>> Starchy or sugary food is eaten
>> This food is digested into glucose
>> Blood glucose levels go up as a result
>> Insulin is secreted from the pancreas
>> Insulin moves glucose away from the blood
>> Blood glucose levels go down

The glycaemic index

You may have heard of the glycaemic index or GI. This is simply a means of rating how different carbohydrate foods affect your blood glucose levels. Carbs that make your blood glucose rise quickly are called high-GI foods. Those that give you slower and steadier blood glucose levels are low-GI foods, so it is important for people with diabetes to eat these more often than high-GI foods.

There is no need for you to know the specific GI rating of different foods, but it is helpful to have some knowledge of the types of foods that are lower in GI so that you can add more of them to your diet. Low-GI foods can also be beneficial in terms of general health, and they are usually higher in fibre than high-GI foods. Because low-GI foods are digested more slowly, some people find that they help to keep them fuller for longer. So choosing to have a low-GI eating plan can help you to control your weight because you may feel less hungry between meals.

Generally, it is best to keep high-GI foods, such as sugar-rich drinks, to a minimum. They make your blood glucose levels rise quickly and tend to offer fewer nutrients as they are often processed. However, there is a use for some high-GI foods in diabetes – and that's when you have low blood glucose levels (see p10).

Although low-GI carbs are healthy, it doesn't mean that you should eat lots of them. They have a beneficial effect on your blood glucose level only if eaten in controlled amounts. If, for example, you choose to eat a huge plateful of basmati rice, your blood glucose is likely to go up quickly, even though the rice is a low-GI food. Therefore it is really important to watch your portion size. Also, cooking a low-GI food in lots of fat will obviously cancel some of the health benefits. For more on portion sizes and healthy cooking methods, turn to pages 20 and 23 respectively.

examples of your low-GI and medium-GI friends

Breads
Granary, multi-grain or seeded
Millet (bajra) roti
Wholemeal coarse chapatis/whole-wheat rotis

Grains and pasta
Cracked/bulgur wheat (lapsi)
Bangladeshi rice
Basmati or easy-cook rice
Al dente (lightly cooked) pasta
Noodles

Breakfast cereals
Porridge
Muesli
Bran cereals, e.g. All-Bran, bran flakes

Starchy vegetables
Sweet potato/Yam
Cassava (mogo)
Raw plantain (green banana)
Beans, e.g. kidney beans, black-eyed beans,
   chickpeas
Lentils, e.g. moong, toor, urad, masoor

Fruits
Fresh fruits, e.g. apples, pears, peaches, oranges,
plums, kiwi fruit, strawberries, cherries, grapes,
mangoes and pineapples
Dried fruits, e.g. sultanas, raisins and apricots

how to eat well

1 Eat regular meals

Eat at regular intervals and make sure that you have three meals a day. This will help your blood glucose level remain steady throughout the day, minimising potentially harmful highs and lows. It also helps you to have good energy levels as the day progresses and prevents you feeling hungry.

2 Choose high-fibre foods

The advantage of high-fibre foods, which are usually low- or medium-GI foods is that they are digested more slowly and therefore produce a slower release of glucose into the bloodstream. But while all high-fibre foods are good for your health, you can't assume that all high-fibre foods help your blood glucose to rise slowly. Wholemeal bread has a high GI rating (like white bread) because although it is high in fibre it is digested quickly because the grains are 'mashed up'. Granary bread has a lower GI since the grains are still whole. Therefore it makes sense to eat high-fibre foods as part of a balanced eating plan and, where possible, to try to choose lower-GI versions.

The benefit of high-fibre foods is greatly increased if they are processed as little as possible. So, for example, eating brown basmati rice is better than eating white rice (which has had the outer husk removed); eating wholegrain rotis is better than eating rotis made from refined white flour; and eating dal in which the lentils are still whole is better than eating dal in which the lentils have been puréed.

You can also improve the amount of fibre in your diet by adding extra beans and vegetables to meat curries and eating at least the recommended five portions of fruit and vegetables a day.

3 Cut down on fried and fatty food

The type of food you choose can affect your blood cholesterol levels. Eating animal or saturated fats (from fatty meat and full-fat dairy products) can raise your 'bad' (or LDL) cholesterol level, which can lead to a build-up of fatty streaks in your arteries, which can in turn reduce the blood flow to your heart. Since people with diabetes are at an increased risk of getting heart disease, it makes sense to watch the amount of fat that you eat. And remember, fried and fatty foods are also high in calories, so if you are trying to manage your weight, cut down on the amount of fat you use and how often you eat fatty foods.

The fried and fatty foods to be wary of include butter, ghee, full-fat cheese (such as paneer), fatty meats, the skin on chicken, vermicelli dessert (seviyan), samosas, pastries and savoury snacks such as bombay mix (chevda) and crisps.

Choose monounsaturated fats (like the fat found in olive and rapeseed oil, avocado, a handful of nuts) or polyunsaturated fats (such as corn oil, sunflower oil, and spreads made from these oils) instead. The recipes in this book will help you to eat less of the harmful saturated fats and substitute them with healthier unsaturated fats as well as try to reduce the overall amount of fat you use.

five ways to eat healthy fats

● Avoid cooking with saturated fats such as butter or ghee. Replace with mono-unsaturated oils preferably (olive, rapeseed) or poly-unsaturated oils (groundnut, corn, sunflower).

● Avoid full-fat dairy products such as cream, paneer and yogurt. Choose skimmed milk and low-fat yogurt instead, and try replacing paneer with tofu.

● Cut down on processed foods, which are often heavy in saturated fat.

● Snack on a small handful of unsalted nuts instead of cakes, biscuits, savoury Indian snacks or mithai.

● Avoid using too much coconut in your cooking. Creamed coconut and coconut milk are high in saturated fat. Use low-fat coconut milk or fresh coconut.

4 Eat oily fish twice a week

Scientific studies suggest that eating oily fish regularly can protect you from developing heart problems. The omega-3 oils found in oily fish have been shown to lower a type of fat in your blood called triglyceride, and they also may help to reduce blood stickiness, so making your blood less likely to clot and cause a blockage in your arteries. Choosing oily fish as part of a healthy diet can therefore help to preserve your heart health.

Examples of oily fish include: salmon, mackerel, trout, sardines and herring. Two Bengali oily fish to look out for are ilish mach (hilsa) and boal mach. If you eat small fish with the bones (such as sardines and mola), you'll also be getting lots of calcium.

5 Eat more fruit and vegetables

These foods are rich in valuable antioxidants, which can help prevent damage to your arteries. Simply by eating a variety of colours you can make sure a good range of antioxidants is included in your diet. For example, you get betacarotene from orange- and yellow-coloured vegetables such as carrots and yellow peppers, and anthocyanin (a powerful antioxidant) from purple fruit and vegetables such as blueberries, red cabbage and beetroot.

Getting into the habit of eating more vegetables with your main meals will benefit your health greatly, since these foods are nutritious, low-GI, often filling, and also low in calories and fat. Make sure that around half your plate is made up of vegetables or salad. If you're not used to this, start by having just a small amount and then build up the quantity gradually. It doesn't have to be complicated: a chopped tomato with some fresh coriander and lemon juice is as simple as it gets.

Indian cuisine is packed with brightly coloured vegetables, from bhindi to brinjal, so there is plenty to enjoy. And if you make one of the tasty recipes in this book, you can be sure that the vegetables are cooked with diabetes in mind.

Like anyone with a healthy diet, always aim to eat at least five servings of fruit and vegetables a day.

fruit and vegetable portions

- 1 apple, banana, pear, orange or other similarly sized fruit
- 2 plums, apricots, satsumas or similarly sized fruit or $\frac{1}{2}$ a grapefruit or avocado
- 1 slice of a large fruit, such as melon, mango, papaya or pineapple
- 3 heaped tablespoons of vegetables (raw, cooked, frozen or tinned but not potatoes or sweet potatoes)
- 3 heaped tablespoons of beans or lentils *
- 3 heaped tablespoons of fruit salad (fresh or tinned in fruit juice) or stewed fruit
- 1 heaped tablespoon of dried fruit (such as raisins or apricots)
- 1 handful of grapes, cherries or berries
- 1 dessert bowl of salad (such as lettuce or other leaves, tomatoes, cucumber etc.)
- 1 glass (150ml) of unsweetened fruit juice *

Those foods marked with an asterisk (*) count as a maximum of one portion a day however much you eat or drink of them.

Dried fruit is relatively high in sugar, so eating too much can compromise blood glucose levels. Only one portion of fruit juice is recommended partly because the valuable fibre has been removed. Also, drinking too much fruit juice, even though it is unsweetened, can cause your blood glucose levels to rise sharply (natural sugar in liquid form is absorbed rapidly into the blood).

five ways to eat more fruit and veg

● Choose fruit or dried fruit as snacks between meals.

● Finish your meal with some fresh fruit instead of mithai.

● Have a salad with your meals – even if it's a sandwich, you can still pile in some lettuce and tomato.

● Keep a snack-attack vegetable box for when you need to eat something but it's not yet time for your meal. Choose any raw vegetables, such as carrots, cucumber, cherry tomatoes, celery or mooli.

● Drink a glass of unsweetened fruit juice with a meal as it counts, once, towards your daily amount.

6 Swap high-sugar for low-sugar

Say the word diabetes and, more often than not, sugar comes to mind. Yet sugar does not cause diabetes nor, when you have diabetes, do you need to avoid sugar completely. Nevertheless, it is still a good rule of thumb to swap foods which are high in sugar for those with a lower sugar content: for example, replace tinned fruit in syrup with tinned fruit in natural juice (the difference in taste is marginal), sugar with artificial sweeteners, and mithai with fresh or dried fruit.

It is worth remembering that if you eat a little sugar mixed with other foods, especially at the end of a high-fibre meal, your blood glucose rises more slowly than if you have, for example, a drink high in sugar on its own. This is because the sugar is digested as part of a meal rather than on its own when it can rapidly enter your bloodstream. So you will find that some recipes in this book use small amounts of sugar, and that's fine. Note, however, that sugary foods often tend to also be high in fat (think of cakes, biscuits, rasmalai and kulfi) and are generally unhealthy, so it's best to eat these only rarely.

If you add sugar to tea or coffee, cut back by half a teaspoonful per cup each week. Your tastes have a strange way of adapting, so you'll find that you will get used to it. Keep going and you'll soon cut out sugar altogether – better for both your waistline and your teeth. Even masala chai can be tasty without sugar.

five ways to eat less sugar

● Replace fizzy drinks with diet ones, unsweetened fruit juice, no added sugar squash or water.

● Limit Indian sweets, such as barfi, jalebi, ladoo, penda and gulab jaman, to special occasions.

● Limit the use of sugar and jaggery or gur in cooking.

● You can use an artificial sweetener such as Canderel, Splenda or Sweetex instead of sugar.

● Avoid condensed milk. Use light evaporated milk instead.

7 Get the balance right

Make sure that you're getting the overall balance of foods right. When you sit down to a meal, look at your plate and check that each part is filled with an appropriate amount of each of the different food groups.

Below is a diagram of the different food groups and how much of each you should aim to have. So, for example, the diagram shows that a large part of your food should be fruit and vegetables, and that healthy carbs are also important. You need to include some dairy foods and protein foods regularly too, as shown. And the smallest part is filled with sugary and fatty foods: these provide little nutritional benefit and can be high in calories so, it's best to save them for special occasions.

healthy eating for the Asian community

For a diet to be healthy it needs to be balanced. This diagram shows you the proportions of the different types of food you should try to eat.

Fruit and Vegetables
Aim for 5 or more servings each day

1 serving = 1 apple,
1 banana,
3 tablespoons of vegetables,
small bowl of salad,
1 small glass of
unsweetened fruit juice

These provide important vitamins, minerals and fibre.

Chapatis/Rotis, Rice and other Cereal
Aim for 4-5 servings each day

1 serving = 1 slice bread,
1 bowl cereal, 1 medium
potato, 2 tablespoons cooked
rice, 2 tablespoons cooked
pasta, I medium chapati/roti

These foods are healthy until oil, butter or margarine are added.

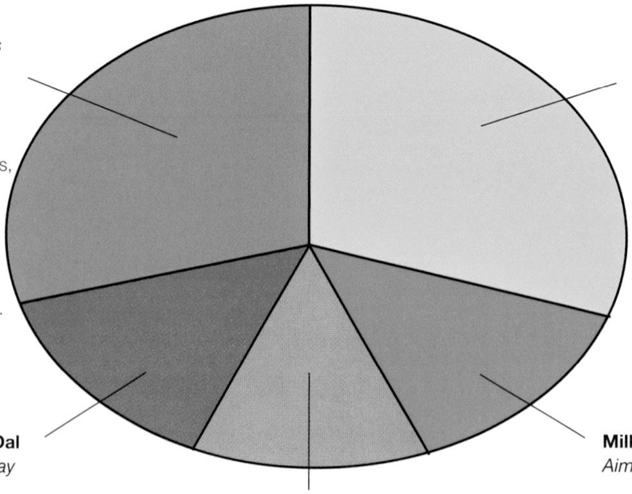

Meat, Fish, Pulses and Dal
Aim for 2 servings each day

1 serving = 75g cooked meat
100g cooked fish
125g cooked beans, lentils
or dal

These are good sources of protein.
Oily fish such as tuna is good for you, try to eat 2 portions a week. Try to cut down on red meat.

Fatty and Sugary Foods

Try not to eat these too often and, when you do, have small amounts. These foods are high in calories and cause weight gain.
Cut down on deep-fried foods like samosas or puri. Cut down on cakes, biscuits and pastries. Avoid sweetened drinks (use diet and unsweetened ones instead).

Milk and Dairy Foods
Aim for 3 servings each day

1 serving = 1/3 pint (200ml) milk
25g hard cheese
1 small pot of yogurt or 1 glass
of lassi
Skimmed or semi-skimmed milk is better than full cream milk.

These provide protein and calcium for healthy bones and teeth.

Adapted with kind permission from Leicestershire Nutrition and Dietetic Service

five ways to eat less salt

● Don't snack on salty foods such as chevda, ganthia, sev, pooris, salted crisps, savoury biscuits and salted nuts. Choose fresh fruit, unsalted nuts and plain popcorn instead.

● Avoid processed and convenience foods since these are often loaded with salt.

● Read food labels carefully: salt may appear as sodium, sodium chloride, monosodium glutamate or bicarbonate of soda. Avoid packaged foods that contain more than 1.5g of salt per 100g (or 0.6g sodium per 100g).

● Taste your food before adding salt at the table and avoid adding any at all if possible. Try adding pepper or other ground spices instead.

● Choose products that have a reduced-salt content, such as unsalted butter.

8 Choose foods which are low in salt

We don't usually measure salt in traditional Indian cooking – it's often a generous pouring straight from the salt container, and we don't think twice about it. However, there is now solid research to show that eating too much salt makes you more at risk of raised blood pressure and strokes.

Salt is the common name for sodium chloride, and it is the sodium part of the compound which is considered to be harmful if taken in excess. Bear in mind that the recommended limit for adults is 6g or less per day: the equivalent of just over a teaspoon.

As you begin to try out the recipes included in this book, you'll notice that they are low in salt yet high in taste – so it is possible to eat healthily and still enjoy fine dining. For more on cooking with less salt, turn to page 28.

9 Go easy on the alcohol

You may have chosen not to drink alcohol for religious or personal reasons. If you do drink, however, here are some useful guidelines.

We advise that women keep to a maximum of two units per day and men three units per day. However, it is better to drink less than this, and, if you are taking certain medications for your diabetes, you must make sure that you eat something with an alcoholic drink, since drinking alcohol on an empty stomach can make your blood glucose fall dangerously low, and can cause hypoglycaemia.

Weight for weight, alcohol contains more calories than sugar, so even moderate drinking can make you gain weight. For example, one pint of beer has around the same calories as three chocolate biscuits. Replacing meals with alcoholic drinks can mean that you lose out on important vitamins and minerals, so it's simply a matter of thinking about how much you drink and when.

Binge drinking or drinking too much can lead to long-term effects such as cancers, memory loss, heart disease and stomach ulcers. It is also known to trigger drops in blood glucose levels (hypos), which are particularly important to avoid if you have diabetes.

Unfortunately for those who need to monitor carefully how much they drink, alcohol by volume and serving sizes have gone up in recent years, particularly in relation to wine. One unit of alcohol used to be 125ml of a wine that contained 8 per cent of alcohol by volume (ABV). Today, a lot of wines sold may contain as much as 13 per cent ABV. Alcohol content makes a big difference to the amount of units you may drink at any one time. For example, a standard glass (175ml) of 13 per cent ABV wine contains 2.3 units, compared to 1.6 units in a standard glass of 9 per cent ABV. To monitor how much you are drinking read the labels on your wine bottles to gauge the wine strength or ask the bartender for the alcohol content of the wine.

You can use the following equation to accurately work out the number of units in your drink:

$$\frac{\text{ABV} \times \text{volume}}{1000} = \text{number of units}$$

1 unit of alcohol is approximately:
$1/2$ pint (284ml) ordinary strength beer, lager or cider
1 pub measure (50ml) sherry, apéritif or liqueur
1 pub measure (25ml) of spirits, e.g. vodka, gin or whisky

10 Avoid special diabetic products
You may see confectionery labelled as 'suitable for diabetics'. Many of these foods have around the same number of calories and the same amount of fat as a non-diabetic version, and they offer you no benefit. These special products are often more expensive, too, and some can have a laxative effect. Save your money – you simply don't need them.

size matters...

What you put on your plate is crucial, but equally important is the size of your portion. There's little value in eating healthy low-GI pasta if it is heaped onto your plate! Here are some tips to help you keep a watchful eye on how much you eat.

● Eat from a smaller plate to make your meals look bigger.

● Look at the amount of food suggested in the recipes in this book – they are designed to serve a family of four. As you get used to the recipes, you'll soon work out how much food is appropriate for one person.

● Get into the habit of serving a salad or vegetable with each meal.

● Have one helping of food – and only one. It takes time to develop this habit, so give yourself (body and mind) a week or two to get used to the idea. If you want more, add more salad or vegetables or have an extra piece of fruit.

● Avoid night-time snacking and TV dinners. Eat at a table and be conscious of what you're eating.

● Distract yourself at times when you feel like over-indulging. Perhaps go for a stroll, take a bath or read a magazine.

● Chat more, sip more water and eat slowly.

it's our culture, we can't help it!

When you invite someone home for a cup of tea, do you just serve tea? Tea and biscuits? Or is it tea, chevda, mithai and more? And, no doubt, when you are invited to dinner, there is a whole array of exciting dishes on the table. Perhaps you will be offered second helpings; in some cases you may even be forced into second helpings by a well-meaning elderly relative. These are just a few examples of good old traditional South Asian hospitality, and generally it's something we should be proud of. There is a beautiful sense of unity and generosity around mealtimes, and although there's nothing wrong with that, making some simple adjustments to your approach to eating and cooking will greatly improve your chances of success when it comes to looking after your health.

Is traditional South Asian cuisine healthy?

Traditional South Asian cooking used to be very healthy. The use of a wide range of healthy foods, from basmati rice and wholegrain chapatis to an array of fresh vegetables, together with comparatively low-fat proteins including beans and lean meats, meant that the South Asian diet was relatively low in fat and high in fibre. However, as communities have become more affluent and westernised, either in their own countries or after emigrating to the West, South Asian cooking has gradually become higher in fat, sugar and calories, and lower in healthy, high-fibre carbohydrate.

Although this isn't a welcome change, the good news is that we know what it takes to be better! Our families and ancestors have traditionally eaten foods that are healthier, and all we need to do is to embrace those traditional habits to enjoy a selection of tasty South Asian delights that are also conducive to good health.

There are so many great aspects to our traditional

cooking, but the reality is that some of the ingredients that we use are not healthy. In fact, many of the ingredients – and especially the amounts used – can actually be harmful in terms of your long-term health. For example, spreading butter or ghee on chapatis, or deep-frying samosas in oil, can add unnecessary fat and calories to your meal. As stated before, too much fat makes you gain weight, and too much saturated fat can raise the levels of 'bad' cholesterol in your blood.

Sadly, the tradition of handing down recipes from mothers and grandmothers is not necessarily a good thing. We all love those home-cooked dishes that only mum can make best. However, it is often the case that these recipes do not contain measured ingredients. Instead, it's a liberal pouring of oil from a container, a fistful of dal and a generous pinch of salt. Where diabetes is concerned, and, in fact, when generally caring for your health, it is important to measure out certain ingredients to help you keep an eye on your calorie, saturated fat, carbohydrate and salt intake.

The liberal use of salt in South Asian cooking is of particular importance since eating too much salt makes you more at risk of high blood pressure and, therefore, heart disease. Since your taste buds are probably accustomed to salty foods, you'll probably need to make the reduction in your use of salt a gradual process. Tell yourself that the other benefit of reducing the salt content in your food is that you will begin to taste all of the other flavours that the salt previously obscured. Furthermore, you will be improving the health of your children: if you cook family meals with less salt, your children will get used to it and they will be less likely to choose high-salt foods in adult life.

The guidance and recipes in this book should help to minimise the less good aspects of Indian cooking and help you to capitalise on the very valuable traditional habits that can be positively health-promoting.

eating out

Restaurants have helped to promote great South Asian cooking around the world, but in the process a lot of traditional dishes have been swept away or changed almost beyond recognition. For example, cream and coconut are often used as a shortcut to making dishes richer and tastier. Both cream and coconut are, of course, high in saturated fat. Nevertheless, there are plenty of traditional dishes that you can enjoy while still keeping an eye on your waistline. Here are some tips for eating out with a guilt-free conscience:

● For the main course, go for a dal dish, which is made from lentils. There are usually many different types to choose from. The more whole the lentils, the lower the GI rating, as the fibre in the lentils has not been mashed up and your digestive system needs to work harder to break it down.

● Opt for chicken, prawn or vegetable dishes since they tend to be lower in fat than those containing red meats. If you're in a restaurant and are confronted with a layer of oil on top of a dish, scoop your serving from underneath.

● If you want to eat chicken, go for tandoori chicken or chicken tikka since these are usually roasted in a tandoor or baked, which means they are cooked without added fat.

● Resist the richer dishes such as korma, pasanda and masala, and deep-fried snacks such as samosas and bhajias/pakoras.

● Accompany your meal with some steamed or boiled basmati rice, and stay away from pilau and biryanis, unless you want to just have a small amount.

● Choose a side salad, even if you're not used to it. Salad will help to fill you up, it provides valuable nutrients and colour, and also fills part of your plate to help you to avoid overdoing it! A simple raita can also make a cooling and low-GI accompaniment.

● Try to resist finishing your meal with kulfi. Regular kulfi is usually made from full-cream milk, cream and sweetened condensed milk – save your calorie allowance for something more nutritious, such as fresh fruit.

healthy cooking tips

Making the right changes to your cooking methods can make a big difference to your overall health.

All the delicious recipes in this book have been created using authentic ingredients and cooking styles, but every ingredient is carefully measured to help you get the best nutritional value from each meal. This doesn't mean that everything you cook must be meticulously weighed. In time, you'll become accustomed to the amount of oil or salt that is added to family meals, so that you will be able to apply the same principles when cooking other dishes.

Use our guide below for tasty ideas on how to make your restaurant meals healthier, especially if you are cooking your favourites at home.

Traditional food	Swap for this	Why?
Butter chicken	Grilled chicken tikka or tandoori chicken	Cream and butter contain lots of saturated fat; the alternative has very little added fat but all the taste.
Lamb curry	Saag lamb (lean)	Lamb can be fatty, but this swap uses lean lamb with all the fat trimmed off and it's bulked up with spinach.
Egg bhurji	Egg bhurji made with extra vegetables	Bulk up the meal with a vegetable side dish of onion, green pepper, tomatoes and mushrooms.
Aloo paratha	Gobi/mixed vegetable paratha, dry roasted	Instead of having a high-carb potato filling, choose a vegetable one and avoid using butter or ghee.
Khichdi	Khichdi made with less rice and more moong	Increase the low-GI lentil portion and avoid adding butter or ghee to keep the fat content down.
Potato curry	Mixed vegetable/bhindi	If having other carbs at the meal (e.g. khichdi, roti or rice), then choose a veg-based curry and skip the potato.
Mattar paneer	Mixed beans/ chickpeas/ tofu curry	Paneer is high in saturated fat, so try a vegetarian protein alternative; the beans are low-GI.
Thepla	Dry-roasted thepla made with no oil or ghee	Frying thepla makes them high in fat, but cooking in a non-stick tawa without added fat will give a crisp and tasty alternative.
Aloo bharta	Gobi mattar	If you are going to have breads or rice with a meal then opt for a vegetable-based curry instead of aloo.
Fried stuffed bhindi	Stuffed bhindi cooked with very little oil	If cooked in a non-stick pan, you can get all the flavours of the traditional dish with much less fat.

Traditional food	Swap for this	Why?
Dal made with ghee	Dal made without ghee	Dal can be low-GI but using ghee or oil increases the fat content and reduces the overall health benefit. Try measuring very little oil or using spray oil.
Medu wada	Steamed idli	Wadas are fried and so high in fat, but steaming idlis keeps the fat content down.
Avial (curry made with creamed coconut)	Curry made with a little fresh cocount	Creamed coconut is high in saturated fat. By using a small amount of fresh coconut you can still get a similar taste and aroma.
Upma	Vegetable upma made with little oil	By bulking up the upma with other vegetables you can reduce the GI of the dish.
Fried samosa	Samosa baked in the oven	Avoid frying to keep the fat content down.
Pakora/bhajia	Handvo/dhokla	Baked or steamed snacks are better than fried.
Fried papad	Papad cooked in the microwave or grilled	You can still get the same taste and crispy texture without frying.
Oily pickles	Vegetable raita made with fat-free yogurt or salad dressed with lemon juice and pepper or chilli	Pickles can be high in salt and fat but the alternatives are lower in fat and also have a low GI.
Rasmalai	Kheer made with skimmed milk	Substitute full-fat milk in desserts for skimmed milk, and sweeten them with dried fruit such as raisins.
Kulfi	Shrikhand made with low-fat Greek-style yogurt	Keep all the taste of saffron and cardamom but in a lower-fat alternative.
Tinned mango pulp	Fruit salad with fresh mango pulp	Keep the sugar intake down and reduce the GI of the dessert with the fresh unsweetened alternative.

Choosing the right fats

As we have seen, healthy eating isn't just about low fat – it's about the right fat and the right balance. But bear in mind that, weight for weight, fat provides twice the calories of starch or protein. Add fat and you bump up the calories: fry an egg and the calories are almost double those of a boiled or poached one.

Tasty food doesn't have to have a lot of fat. You can spice up your dishes with traditional flavourings like herbs (coriander, fenugreek and dill) and spices (chilli, cumin, etc.), which are fat free. Nor does reducing the amount of fat in your food have to be a complicated business. Instead of undermining the benefits of a healthy salad by dressing it in lots of oil, you can add flavour by using nothing but lime or lemon juice (and the acid from the citric juice can help lower the GI of the meal, too!).

Here are some tips for reducing the fat in your cooking:

● If you need to fry onions and spices or make a tarka, try spraying oil on a non-stick pan. Oil spray bottles enable you to use a fraction of the oil you would normally. If spraying oil just doesn't do it for you, use a measured amount of rapeseed or olive oil: around 1 tablespoonful for a dish for four people.

● After frying spices, pour off any extra oil before you continue cooking.

● When you finish cooking, check whether you could drain off some oil from the top of the pan before serving. You might like to try using a piece of kitchen paper to blot the oil off.

● Select lean cuts of meat and trim off any visible fat. Try to cook meat without adding any extra fat: for example, by grilling, roasting or baking.

● Remove the skin from poultry and remember that the thigh and leg meat has the highest fat content.

● Eggs can be poached, boiled or scrambled instead of fried. Unless you have been told to avoid eggs for a medical reason, you can eat 5–6 eggs per week.

● Avoid high-fat sauces (such as korma) and dishes which contain a lot of butter, cream or oil. Experiment with reduced-fat foods, such as low-fat yogurt, semi-skimmed milk, reduced-fat coconut milk or skimmed milk powder.

● Go easy on the cheese. Paneer contains saturated fat, so if you cook with it, use less fat in other accompanying dishes. Or try replacing it with tofu.

● Use low-fat alternatives to milk products, such as low-fat yogurt and skimmed milk.

● Consider chapatis without butter or ghee – do you really need extra fat if you're going to be scooping up a tasty curry? If you really *must* spread fat on your chapatis, try spreading it on alternate ones only (you'll find that the fat will keep both chapatis moist) and use an olive oil-based spread instead of butter or ghee.

● Bake samosas – simply brush them with a little oil and bake on foil in a roasting tray. They will be browned and crispy but much lower in fat than the fried version.

If you are planning to cook with less oil, it is worth investing in a non-stick pan or two. Using non-stick pans for cooking curries, or a non-stick tawa for cooking breads, is a great way to reduce the need for extra fat. If you are using conventional pans, cooking with less oil may cause the food to stick. You can avoid this by cooking on a lower heat or by adding small amounts of water.

Choosing the right carbs

Although carbohydrates are healthy as part of a balanced diet, the amount that you eat will affect your overall health, as well as your blood glucose levels. As you will have seen from the plate model on page 18, you need to have only four to five servings of carbohydrate foods each day to maintain good health. Choosing to eat lots of rice and chapatis (wholegrain or not) morning, noon and night is not the right approach. Nor is, for example, combining a potato curry, chapati and rice on one plate: too much carbohydrate at once will make your blood glucose levels rise quickly, which is undesirable.

Try to choose a low- or medium-GI food for every meal or snack. Your blood glucose will be better controlled if you spread your intake of carbs throughout the day rather than if you save it all up for your main meal. These starchy foods should help to fill you up, and tend to be lower in calories than fatty foods. You do, however, need to watch your portion sizes (see page 20).

Here are some tips for incorporating healthy carbs into your cooking:

● Base your meal around a low-GI carbohydrate – such as basmati rice, noodles, sweet potato, or grains such as cracked wheat (lapsi, unsweetened).

● Bangladeshi rice is the rice with the lowest GI (owing to a number of factors, including how the grain is made up). Otherwise basmati rice is good. And choose brown rice as often as you can as this is slower to digest.

● Try cooking with different types of grains, such as cracked/bulgur wheat (lapsi), sorghum (jowar) and millet (bajra). These have a lower GI than rice.

● Keep your carbs, such as dals, as whole as possible rather than puréed, since this helps to lower the GI.

● Make sure that you include generous amounts of vegetables or salad, and ideally both. Remember that fresh, frozen, dried or canned vegetables all count towards your target of a minimum of five-a-day. If you cook your vegetables lightly, they are likely to be more slowly digested, which will lower their GI rating too. Eating your vegetables raw is even better!

● Adding vegetables and beans or lentils to meat dishes will reduce the GI and make them more filling.

● Beans, lentils, sweetcorn and peas are an excellent source of soluble fibre, which has been shown to lower blood cholesterol. Make them a regular part of your diet. They are cheap and nutritious and can make main-meal dishes go further.

● Prepare fresh fruit for puddings rather than sweet desserts or mithai. The fructose in fruit is less damaging to your teeth and to your blood glucose levels than the sucrose (white sugar) used in desserts and sweets, and you won't get any fat from fruits.

Quick tip: Eating carbohydrates makes your blood glucose levels rise – they are important, but choose the right types for slow, steady blood glucose levels

Beware the salt

Given that throwing over-generous amounts of salt into the cooking pot is such a part of traditional Indian cooking (see page 19), this is a habit that you may have to make a big effort to overcome. As you know by now, eating too much salt puts you more at risk of high blood pressure and, therefore, heart disease.

Don't expect to be able to cut out salt altogether, or reduce it drastically overnight. Chances are, if you did that, it wouldn't last and you'd go back to adding the large amounts you once did. Instead, reduce the amount of salt you use in cooking gradually. The recipes in this book will show you how to cook with smaller amounts of salt than you may be used to, and below are some other tips to help you.

● Measure the amount of salt you add during cooking with a teaspoon, and gradually use less.

● Try using less salt by experimenting with new flavours such as fresh herbs, whole and ground spices, freshly ground black pepper and paprika. Also try lime juice, balsamic vinegar and chilli sauce.

● Experiment with low-salt products, such as tinned vegetables in water (rather than brine), and unsalted butter, which can be used as replacements for salt-rich foods.

● Dried fish is very high in salt. Soak it twice and throw away the soaking water before cooking.

● Seasonings and stocks are usually very salty. If you do use them, use a little and note that there is no need to add extra salt in cooking.

meet Mr Rai

Mr Kishan Rai is a 49-year-old Indian man who has recently been diagnosed with Type 2 diabetes. He has lived in London for 20 years and has an appointment with a diabetes specialist dietitian for advice on his eating plan. Mr Rai is approximately 15kg (2 stone 5lb) overweight and his waist measures 96cm (36 inches). That puts him in a BMI (body mass index) category of 30, which is very high risk, and he has a risky waist measurement, too. He is on medication to control his blood pressure, but Mr Rai has no evidence of coronary heart disease or any family history of diabetes.

Mr Rai is not very physically active and his exercise consists of about two hours of walking around the house per week. His blood glucose is not very well controlled.

The dietitian, Alisha, asks him to go through a typical day's meals so she can assess his eating habits. Mr Rai's 'diet history' reveals that he usually eats the following meals:

Meal	Food	How much?
Breakfast	White bread toast	2 slices with butter
	Cup of tea with full-fat milk and sugar	1 teaspoon sugar
	Egg fried in butter	2 (average of 8 eggs per week)
Lunch	Chapati with butter	3 large
	Lamb and potato curry	1 large serving
	Salad	1 small bowl
Mid-evening	Cup of tea (as above)	1
	Sweet biscuits	2–3
Dinner	Pilau rice	1 plate (approx. 400g, boiled)
	Chapati with butter	2 large
	Dal (with ghee used in the tarka)	1 small bowl
	Vegetable curry cooked in oil, and oily pickle	1 small bowl, 2 tablespoons
Post-dinner	Apple	1
	Barfi or ladoo	1 piece

What do you think the dietitian might advise?
Have a go at writing down some changes to the meals Mr Rai chooses.

After the evaluation, Alisha first explains to Mr Rai the importance of diet and lifestyle modification for controlling blood glucose levels (including weight control and physical activity). Understanding why food is important will help him to take more care of his eating habits and be motivated to change. She then goes on to make several suggestions as to changes he can make, using the latest recommendations for diabetes and overall health:

● She advises him to change from white bread to granary or seeded bread since the latter has a lower GI, as well as more fibre and B vitamins.

● He should incorporate healthier breakfast options, such as wholegrain cereals, porridge and muesli.

● He needs to cut down on his portion sizes of carbohydrate foods such as rice, potatoes and chapatis. He needs some carbs, but too many at once can increase the 'glycaemic load', which means his blood glucose rises more quickly.

● He should change from full-fat milk to semi-skimmed milk to cut down on his saturated fat intake.

● He must aim for at least five portions of fruit and vegetables every day, ensuring that he chooses a variety of types. Have fruit as a snack between meals. It's a good idea not to overcook vegetables in a curry: it increases the GI and also reduces the nutrient content.

● He should enjoy other low-GI foods, such as basmati rice and dal.

● He should cook with a monounsaturated oil, such as olive or rapeseed (canola) oil rather than butter or ghee.

● He must avoid adding butter to chapatis and choose lean meats.

Here's what Mr Rai's typical meals look like now:

Meal	Food	How much?
Breakfast	Porridge oats made with semi-skimmed milk,	6 tablespoons 200ml
	OR Boiled egg (no more than 6 per week) and granary bread	2 eggs 2 slices
	Tea with semi-skimmed milk, no sugar	1 cup
	Glass of unsweetened fruit juice or a piece of fruit	1
Mid-morning	Fruit or low-fat yogurt	1 fruit or 1 small carton
Lunch	Chapati made with wholewheat flour, no added butter	2 (each around 40g), the size of a saucer
	Lean lamb curry with spinach OR chicken (with skin removed before cooking), made with 1 tablespoon oil for 4 people	1 bowl (2–3 pieces of meat, around 100g)
	Salad (lime juice and black pepper dressing)	1 bowl
	Low-fat yogurt raita	a few tablespoons
	Fresh fruit	1
Mid-afternoon	Tea with semi-skimmed milk, no sugar	1 cup
	High-fibre crackers OR oatcakes,	2
	OR unsalted almonds	10–12
Dinner	Basmati rice, boiled (no added fat)	1 small bowl (200g cooked)
	Chapati made with wholewheat flour (OR 2 small potatoes included in the veg curry below)	1 (around 40g), the size of a saucer
	Bean and vegetable curry made with 1 tablespoon oil for 4 people	1 small bowl
	Dal or lentil curry using spray oil for tarka	1 bowl
	Chutney or pickle made without oil	1 tablespoon
Post-dinner	Fruit	1

Now Mr Rai's daily diet offers him far more fibre, three servings of calcium-rich dairy foods, plenty of low-GI carbs such as porridge, nuts, dals and beans, and at least five fruit and vegetable portions. He is eating less carbohydrate as a result of choosing smaller portion sizes of starchy foods like rice, potatoes and chapatis. He is losing weight slowly but steadily, he is a little more active as he goes for a 20-minute walk four times a week, and his blood glucose levels are much more stable. Even his family's overall diet has improved.

What could you take on board from Mr Rai's experience?

managing your weight

There was a time when the ideal shape for a woman on the Bollywood screen was curvaceous. Now, there is increasing pressure for women to be slim. Interestingly, though, as people have become hooked on diets – or at least the idea of them – we seem to be getting more overweight!

Of course, whether you are male or female, it's normal to put on weight as you get older, even if you are eating the same amount and exercising to the same level. The reality is, however, that many people are overweight because of their poor diet and/or lack of exercise. It is well-known that we tend to be less active than we used to be. If you are less active, you burn fewer calories. And if you eat more calories, the end result is that you put on more weight. For those with diabetes, this makes the condition much more difficult to control.

What's important in maintaining a healthy weight – as well as a healthy lifestyle – is to eat well, in the right proportions, and to be moderately active. There is no need for you to go on any special diet as a good eating plan for people with diabetes is the same as a healthy eating plan for the rest of the population. The recipes and tips in this book will help you to lose weight slowly and keep it off.

Not everyone with Type 2 diabetes needs to lose weight. But what about you? Could you do with losing a kilo or two, or perhaps more? You know that you feel better when you are a healthy weight, as it's easier to move around and keep your energy levels up throughout the day. Many people feel more attractive when they are less heavy, too, but what's more significant is that excess weight can be harmful to your long-term health. When you have diabetes, being overweight, especially around the tummy, can complicate matters. Earlier in this book (see page 8) we discussed how being an 'apple' shape can lead to insulin resistance, which could have caused your diabetes in the first place. There is research to show that insulin resistance also makes you more at risk of heart disease.

Your body weight as well as your shape is likely to affect your health. The body mass index (BMI) is used by dietitians and doctors to assess whether your weight could be putting your health at risk. You can easily work out your own BMI by taking your weight in kilograms and dividing it by your height in metres squared. As an example, if you weigh 80kg and are 1.9m tall, you need to divide 80 by [1.9 x 1.9]. The answer is 22.1. Don't be daunted by this sum – it's easy to work out the answer if you use a calculator! The most desirable range is a BMI of between 20 and 24. A larger BMI is taken as an indication of being overweight. The higher the figure, the more overweight you are.

For most overweight people, the good news is that losing just 5 to 10 per cent of your weight can make a significant difference to your blood pressure, blood fat and blood glucose levels. Take a look at the list of benefits from losing just this amount of weight:

- reduced blood pressure
- more than 30 per cent less chance of dying from a diabetes-related problem
- improved blood glucose levels
- reduced 'bad' blood cholesterol (LDL)
- reduced blood triglyceride (another type of harmful fat in the blood)
- raised 'good' blood cholesterol (HDL)
- easier to move around
- improved self-confidence and self-esteem
- better sleeping patterns

- improvement in back and joint pain
- less risk of angina

I hope that by now you are convinced that being a healthy weight makes sense. In which case, let's get started with how you can do something about it, for the sake of your looks, your fitness and your overall health.

Seeking professional advice

It is always better to have professional guidance to help you lose weight when you have diabetes, particularly if your BMI is over 30, which puts you in the 'very high risk' category. If you have not already seen a registered dietitian, simply ask your doctor to refer you to a dietitian at the local hospital or within your doctor's practice. He or she will be able to assess your eating patterns and guide you through a sensible weight-loss plan.

Choosing a goal

You may have tried to lose weight before. Did it work? The chances are it did to start with, and then the weight just crept back on again. In fact, people tend to become more overweight after going on a string of diets. This so-called yo-yo dieting can be more harmful to your health than being slightly overweight in the first place.

The first thing to do is to think hard about what your goal is, either short-term or long-term. You may have decided on a goal with your diabetes healthcare team. Or, you may have noticed that you have an unhealthy waist measurement or BMI and have decided to do something about it. Decide on a long-term target and make it realistic and achievable. If you choose to reduce your weight by 5 per cent of your body weight as your long-term goal, set yourself short-term goals to begin with. Hopefully you can adjust even your long-term goal once you have reached the target weight.

The 5-to-10-per-cent goal

Losing just 5 to 10 per cent of your weight can make a significant difference to your health. It is easy to work out what 5 per cent of your weight is. If, for example, you currently weigh 80kg, 10 per cent of this would be 8kg and 5 per cent would be 4kg. It is realistic and sensible to aim to lose 0.5 to 1kg of weight each week. So, realistically, you could lose 4kg in four to eight weeks. Don't be tempted to try to lose weight more quickly than this, because if you are too strict with yourself the chances are you will simply regain it.

How to win the mind game

When you tell yourself you're on a diet, what thoughts and feelings does this conjure up? Probably feelings of deprivation. You probably want to eat more as a result, and may even choose the wrong things to make yourself feel better. Instead, try saying to yourself that you're living a healthy lifestyle because you want to be healthier, fitter, more energetic and slimmer.

One of the biggest drawbacks of any weight-loss plan is lack of motivation. You can only be motivated when you really believe that you will get something worthwhile as a result of your efforts. Here is your treasure chest of willpower boosters that will help you to stay on track.

1 Decide what's really important

Take a moment to ask yourself what is important to you. Is it your looks, your health? Is it your family, your reputation, your status in the community? Once you truly know what you want in life, you'll be more able and likely to achieve it. How does looking after your diabetes fit in with what is important? When you're making a choice between a piece of fruit and a chunk of chocolate, ask yourself which is going to get you closer to what really matters to you. Choose wisely.

2 Think healthy to become healthy

If you begin to think of yourself as an energetic and healthy person, you are far more likely to make choices that are in line with this belief. For example, more often than not you'll choose the juicy apple over the sticky jalebi because it fits in with your belief of being a healthy person in control of yourself and your choices. This gets easier as you practise it.

3 Walk like a fitter person

Simply by standing tall, with your shoulders back, and a smile on your face, you're more likely to make choices that nourish your new-found self-confident pose.

4 Banish negative thoughts

Get rid of negative 'self talk'. This means stop putting yourself down at every opportunity. We all have a voice in our head that talks down to us. For example, when you've reached for that extra plate of food and know you shouldn't have, you might punish yourself internally as a result. This negative self talk can be extremely demotivating. So, listen to that voice in your head and try, over time, to turn it into a positive force. Of course, if you are making healthier choices, there'll be nothing negative for the voice to tell you!

5 Get others on board

There may be some stigma attached to diabetes within your community. Some people prefer not to tell others that they have diabetes. This can make it difficult because it's harder to refuse unhealthy foods when you don't really have an excuse. If you're trying to be healthy and the rest of the family does not support you, you can feel isolated, and this can affect the amount of effort you put in to managing your diabetes.

You are going to have to make lifestyle decisions in your everyday life, and it will be far easier for you if you surround yourself with people who respect that. Of course, there are social and cultural pressures, but family support can have benefits not only for you, but also for the community at large.

Increase your chances of success

You will increase your chances of losing weight if you have some strategies that you can make use of on a daily basis.

● Make a list of all the benefits of reaching your target weight. This might focus on achieving specific health targets, such as improved blood glucose or cholesterol levels. Or it might simply cover things that you would be able to do more easily if you were less heavy: for example, being able to run for a train or bus, get up from a comfortable sofa more easily, go up and down the stairs, run with your children or grandchildren in the park, get into the clothes you've dreamed about wearing for years, and so on. This list can be very motivating, so keep it handy.

● Try putting up a picture of how you'd like to look – this may be an old photo of yourself – on the fridge or somewhere else where you can look at it often. As well as giving you something visual to focus on, the photo will act as a reminder of what you can achieve.

● Reward yourself when you achieve each short-term goal, as giving yourself a mental boost will encourage you to carry on. Go out with friends to see a new

Bollywood blockbuster, or take a trip to the theatre, or simply treat yourself to a new book or DVD.

● Weigh yourself only once a week. Your weight fluctuates from day to day and it is not helpful to weigh yourself more often. And be patient: it took time to put on the weight, and getting it off will take time, too. Being patient will also help you keep the weight off in the longer-term.

● Never shop when you're hungry or you might go for those quick-fix snacks and regret it later. And take a shopping list, so you don't get tempted by food that you don't need to buy.

...and on days when you feel it's hard work, take a look at your list of how great you'll feel when you get there and simply start again. You're only human, and it's all right to have those 'off' days.

Counting the calories

Getting down to a healthy weight will happen only if you make changes to the way you eat and if you reduce the number of calories that you take in as food. We obviously need some calories in order to be able to move around and perform our daily tasks.

Almost all food and drink provides calories, but it is better to get your calories from certain foods (such as low-fat dairy products, low-GI carbs, fruit and vegetables) than others (high-sugar and high-fat foods such as cakes, biscuits, desserts and mithai). This is because the healthier foods will provide you with a range of nutrients that keep your body in optimum condition. Furthermore, these foods will help you to manage your blood glucose and fat levels.

A ground-breaking research project carried out by King's College, London, and supported by the UK Department of Health and the Aga Khan Health Board was published in 2000. This research compared the nutrient content of cooked foods within different South Asian groups in the UK. For the first time, healthcare professionals were able to have a comprehensive insight into foods cooked by UK South Asian households and their nutritional value.

From this and other data, we can estimate the calorie values of common foods; they can only be an estimate because cooking methods in South Asian communities vary widely. Even two people in the same household will cook the same meal differently. The chart below gives the average calorie values of a few traditional foods and compares them with the values of some high-fat foods as well as healthy alternatives.

No doubt you've eaten all the foods listed in the first column (and probably more) in one sitting, perhaps at a celebration. So consider this: that particular meal

Food	Estimated calories	Equivalent to fatty foods	Equivalent to healthy foods
Meat samosa	About 250 cals each	Regular portion of chips	Bowl of cereal with semi-skimmed milk
Pakora or bhajia	100–150 cals each	1–2 spring rolls	2 slices of bread
Matar paneer	About 600 cals (200g portion)	Bowl of chevda (125g)	12 tablespoons dal (using little oil)
1 chapati with ghee	200 cals (depends on size)	3 chocolate biscuits	3 slices of bread, no butter
Plate of biryani	About 800 cals (400g portion)	2–3 doughnuts	14 tablespoons boiled rice (580g portion)
Piece of mithai	200–300 cals each	All-butter croissant	4–6 apples

Half the plate is filled with chicken curry, the other half with rice and rotis

A quarter chicken curry, a quarter vegetable curry, a quarter rice and roti and a quarter salad for a much healthier diet

gives you around 2,200 calories, which is the amount recommended for an adult woman for the whole day! And to look at one example in more detail, the filling in a samosa is usually made from meat or a masala vegetable, both of which contain fat. And then the filled pastry is fried, adding yet more fat! And do you ever eat just one samosa? Be honest with yourself. Knowing that each samosa gives you the about same calories as a portion of chips might make you think twice next time. And look carefully at column 4, which shows you a healthier food with the same number of calories as the high-fat foods. See how much more of the healthier food you can eat to get the same number of calories.

Cutting the calories

By simply cutting a few calories at every meal, you will be making a real calorie saving by the end of the week. If you can cut down on 500 calories each day, you are able to lose half a kilo of body fat in a week. The recipes in this book are likely to be much lower in calories than your usual recipes, so they will give you a head start.

Another good starting-point for cutting the calories is simply to change what your plate looks like. If you take on this advice, you are likely to lose weight, increase your low-GI carbs and increase your fibre, vitamin and mineral intake, all in one go. The idea is to fill half your plate with a vegetable dish, and a salad or vegetable chutney; a quarter with a starchy food such as rice, a potato dish or a roti; and the last quarter with protein, which could be meat, cheese, fish, eggs or dal.

It is especially important to reduce the amount of carbohydrate you eat. This means having smaller amounts of bread, rice, roti and potatoes. If you're planning to have both rotis and rice with your curries, try telling yourself that just one of these is enough. The meal plans on page 45 provide a guideline as to appropriate meal combinations.

As well as changing the appearance of your plate, it's also a good idea to reduce the size of your plate: there's no easier way to cut down on your portion sizes.

Good habits

We often focus on what we should be eating and forget the importance of how to eat and of the mental processes that help us reach our goals. Eating tends to be something we do without thinking, and this can mean we go on eating without thinking about whether or not we are full. When you are not conscious of what and how much you're eating, you're more likely to overdo it. In diabetes, overdoing it can lead to high blood glucose levels.

Your practical approach to the day-to-day reality of eating healthily is really important. Below are some tips on how to help yourself through the process:

● Eat regular meals three times a day. This helps to avoid hunger pangs between meals, and reduces the need to snack on unhealthy temptations: snacking too much or on the wrong things will slow down any progress you are making.

● Most people have dinner as their main meal of the day. In fact, it is better to eat a lighter meal in the evening. If this is not practical for you, however, try to finish eating dinner around four hours before you go to bed. This will help to give your body time to digest your meal and use up the calories from your food before your metabolism starts to slow down during the night.

● Eat only when you're hungry, not just because you're bored, tired or in a social setting. If you are tempted to eat between meals, ask yourself if you're really hungry. We often eat just because we see food or because it's time to eat. Press that pause button in your mind.

● Give food your full attention and enjoy every mouthful. Be aware of what's on your plate, of the size of bite you're about to take, of the chewing action in your mouth, and of swallowing. Savour the flavours and take it nice and slowly. There's no need to be preparing the next handful or forkful of food until you've finished swallowing. This process will make you feel more satisfied and you'll be less likely to overeat.

● Take the time to sit down and enjoy your meals at a table rather than in front of the TV. This helps you to concentrate while you're eating, and to be aware of the signals from your brain telling you to stop. Did you know that it takes around 15 minutes for your brain to realise that your stomach is full? So if you eat slowly and consciously, you'll give your brain a chance to talk to you!

● Think about the value that food brings you, not only the pleasure. For example, be aware of the various vitamins and minerals that energise you from fruit and vegetables that you eat, the fibre from whole grains that helps you to have a healthy digestion, the omega-3 fats from oily fish that help to keep your heart healthy, and so on. Similarly, imagine the harmful effects of sugar-rich food and drinks on your blood glucose and how butter and ghee make your blood cholesterol go up and clog your blood vessels.

● Have a healthy relationship with food. Don't use food as a reward or for emotional support. Rather, use it and enjoy it as nourishment and sustenance.

● When you deny yourself your favourite food, it often becomes more desirable. Think of children who are told not to eat sweets – you'll find that they will over-indulge at every opportunity. So it is acceptable to allow yourself small amounts of your favourite foods, even if they fall into the fatty and sugary foods section of the plate model (page 18) – as long as you are conscious of what you're doing.

● Finally, make sure that you know about the effects on your body of any food that you eat. Read the guidelines in this book, and use the recipes to help you make tasty meals using low-fat foods and lower-fat cooking methods.

your weight-loss checklist

● Work out and write down your 5 per cent target.

● Decide on a realistic date when you will achieve this weight loss.

● List the benefits of this new weight and refer to them often.

● Be conscious of how often you eat and of your portion sizes.

● Increase your activity levels until you're moderately active for 30 minutes at least five times a week.

Getting physical

If you want to lose weight, you need to eat less and/or be more physically active. Doing a combination of the two is the ideal, and it will give you faster and better results.

Calories or energy are provided by food, so you will gain weight if you eat more than you need for your daily activities. It makes sense, then, that if you exercise more, you will need more energy as you will be using up more calories, and this will help you to lose weight faster. Note that if you are physically inactive, you may want to check with your doctor before starting an exercise routine.

Regular physical activity isn't just about weight loss, however. There's a whole host of benefits, including

bringing oxygen to all parts of your body so you feel more energised; releasing the 'happy' hormones called endorphins which help you to cope with stress; toning up your muscles and encouraging good posture; and, most of all, exercise is recommended to help maintain good overall health and reduce the risks of cancer and heart disease.

So find ways of making activity part of your daily life. Make it fun and make it regular. Being active will make you feel good about yourself and will help you to stay on track with your healthy eating plan. Build up to 30 minutes of moderately intense activity at least five times a week.

● Begin gradually if you're not used to being active. This might mean going up and down the stairs a few times, or walking round the block.

● Incorporate exercise into your daily routine. This could be as simple as walking to get something rather than expecting someone else to get it for you, or jogging in front of your favourite TV drama or soap.

● Be realistic about your own ability. There's no point in enrolling at a gym right at the start if you know it will be a huge struggle. Leave this until you're fitter. If you're not someone who can go to the gym three times a week, you may prefer to walk to work, go swimming with your children, do a bit of gardening at the weekend, or go dancing with a friend. Bhangra and raas-garba are excellent ways to keep fit while you're having fun.

● Even being active in 10–15-minute chunks is cardio-protective, if you start to feel warm and slightly out of breath (you should still be able to hold a conversation).

fasting and diabetes

It is possible to fast safely if you're careful about managing your diabetes. The reason why you need to take care is that some drugs used to treat Type 2 diabetes (sulphonylureas) and insulin can make your blood glucose level drop too low when you are not eating. Not drinking enough water can also make your body dehydrated.

Before you undertake a fast, it's best to speak to your diabetes healthcare team so that they can check how well your diabetes is controlled. If they are concerned that there may be signs of damage to your body as a result of long-term high blood glucose levels, they may recommend that you don't fast. The following advice focuses on Ramadan, but holds for all fasts.

During Ramadan, meals are eaten at Sehri and at the end of the fast, Iftar. Often the evening meal contains lots of carbs and perhaps sugary drinks. Because this is the time when families eat together to break the fast, the food is richer than food you may be eating normally. And you may feel that, having fasted all day, you have an excuse to reward yourself with mithai or sugary drinks. However, these can make your blood glucose level rise unnecessarily quickly.

It's always best to eat more slow-burn carbohydrates which have a low GI. Starchy foods like rice, rotis, naan or potatoes will help to get your blood glucose up more slowly and stop you feeling hungry. Make sure that you have lots of fruit and vegetables, and dal, as these are slowly digested and help your blood glucose to rise more slowly, too.

Breaking the routine of a healthy eating regime in order to fast can provide an excuse to abandon all your hard work, so you need to be particularly strong-willed at this time. Try your best to continue keeping to the advice in this book – you will find the recipes tempting whether or not it is a fasting period!

fasting checklist

● Do not stop taking your medication. Seek the advice of your healthcare team before starting and at the end of the fast, since they may advise you to change the times or amount of medication you take.

● Avoid eating lots of unhealthy foods, no matter how much you may feel like you need a reward. Try to maintain a healthy eating pattern after you break the fast and remember to drink plenty of fluids to prevent you feeling dehydrated.

● Divide your daily food intake into two equal portions, one to be taken at Sehri and one at Iftar.

● Remember to check your glucose level regularly, at least once a day at different times of the day. This will help you to keep an eye on your diabetes.

● After the period of Ramadan, it is essential that you visit your doctor to make sure that your blood glucose is being controlled adequately and also to check whether your medication needs to be adjusted.

complementary and alternative therapies

'A true doctor first tries to treat the disease by food; only when food fails does he prescribe medicines.'

This is a quote from the 6th century, but the philosophy is true for supporters of complementary and alternative therapies in the present day. Natural remedies are often used to treat disease, especially in India. However, it is important to note that your diabetes may well need medication, and trying out other therapies without the advice of your doctor can be counter-productive.

Complementary therapies are taken alongside conventional medicine, whereas alternative therapies are used instead of traditional medicine. There is no strong evidence to back up the claims made regarding many of these therapies, and more research is required, but they are still popular since they are based on cultural beliefs passed down from friends and family.

This section looks at various types of complementary and alternative therapies used to treat diabetes. It is not designed to provide a comprehensive picture but is offered as a brief introduction. If you are tempted by any of the therapies described, go only to a trained therapist and ideally ask your doctor for a recommendation.

Ayurveda

Ayurvedic medicine is a system of diagnosis and treatment that has been practised in India for more than 5,000 years. The term 'ayurveda' comes from Sanskrit ayur meaning 'life' and veda meaning 'knowledge'. Ayurvedic philosophy encourages a balance of the body, mind and spirit to help prevent illness and promote wellness. It teaches that three basic energies, or doshas, exist in everything in the universe and influence all mental and physical processes. We are all born with a particular balance of the three doshas, and it is said that illness occurs when they are not in balance. So the main aim of ayurveda is to maintain or recapture the balance. The ayurvedic management of diabetes is based on the use of natural remedies and exercise.

Home remedies

There are many herbs, spices and oils that are traditionally believed to be beneficial for managing diabetes. For many years, diabetes has been treated with plant medicines. In fact, metformin, which is a widely used treatment for diabetes, has plant origins.

Even though there is very little scientific evidence to prove the effect of natural remedies, and no real indication of long-term safety, most are considered harmless. Nevertheless, it is important that you inform your healthcare team if you are taking, or intending to take, any natural remedies. Since these may interact with your conventional diabetes treatment, your medication may need to be adjusted.

Below are some of the natural remedies:

Fenugreek (methi)
Fenugreek seeds have been shown to lower blood glucose and cholesterol levels and they may also have an 'insulin-type' effect. However, similarly to karela, fenugreek seeds may increase the action of some diabetes medication and so care needs to be taken to avoid low blood glucose levels.

Ivy gourd (tindora/tindli)
It has been suggested that tindora, or tindli, a gherkin-like vegetable, may lower blood glucose levels by affecting the breakdown of glucose in the body and have an 'insulin-type' effect.

Bitter gourd (karela)

Karela has been used widely as a natural remedy for diabetes. Unfortunately, karela curry doesn't do the trick! Research has shown that the fresh juice or extract of the unripe fruit can improve how well you manage glucose levels in your blood. Also, it has been shown that karela may have an 'insulin-type' effect in the body. It may be tempting to try drinking karela juice to help keep your blood glucose levels steady – and that's generally okay, but make sure that you let your doctor know. People taking hypoglycaemic drugs (such as gliclizide) or insulin should use karela with caution as severe low blood glucose levels may result.

Onion and garlic

These have been shown to have therapeutic effects in terms of lowering blood glucose levels and thinning the blood.

Holy basil (tulsi)

This is a herb which may have positive effects on lowering both fasting and after-meal glucose levels.

Guar (cluster bean)

There is good research to show that guar gum, from the vegetable guar, can help lower blood glucose levels. However, eating it fried in a curry will not give you enough to have any significant benefit. That is why pharmaceutical preparations have now been introduced that provide guar gum for its blood glucose lowering effect.

Cinnamon

Recent research has suggested that cinnamon powder may improve blood glucose levels and blood fats in people with diabetes.

Yoga

The word yoga means 'union' in Sanskrit, and is considered to be the union between the mind, body and spirit. Yoga combines physical activity, using various stretches and postures, with relaxation and breathing exercises. There is some evidence that yoga may offer help in managing diabetes by improving glucose tolerance and the body's sensitivity to insulin. It's also a great way to engage in gentle exercise while you look after other aspects of your lifestyle.

Biofeedback

This relaxation technique helps a person to become more aware of, and to learn to deal with, the body's response to pain. Biofeedback emphasises relaxation and stress-reduction techniques, and it has been suggested that the process of stress reduction may lower blood glucose levels.

Guided imagery

This is a relaxation technique that has been widely written about. To practise it, you need to think of peaceful mental images which may also include images

you and your family

of controlling or curing a chronic disease, such as diabetes. You might imagine your insulin working well and moving glucose effortlessly into your muscles. Or you might imagine your arteries being healthy, with no furring, and blood following smoothly through them. People using this technique believe that their condition can be eased with the help of such positive images.

Massage, acupressure and acupuncture

Some research has suggested that massage may have a positive effect on blood glucose levels and symptoms of diabetic neuropathy (nerve damage). This must be done with caution, however, since massage at injection sites may increase insulin absorption and also the risk of hypoglycaemia.

Acupressure and acupuncture are oriental therapies which use certain points on the surface of the body to influence internal organs. In acupuncture, specific points are pierced with needles, while in acupressure the same points are stimulated by deep pressure with a finger-tip or a blunt object. It is believed that acupuncture can help people with diabetes by affecting the body's natural glucose production and so lowering blood glucose. Such therapies may also help specific symptoms and complications of diabetes, such as neuropathy.

Homeopathy

In homeopathy, the symptoms of an illness are often seen as a direct result of the body's attempt to heal itself. So, the purpose of homeopathic remedies is to try to stimulate the body to release its own healing forces. Chromium is a supplement which is often encouraged as a homeopathic remedy for diabetes because of its role in glucose metabolism in the body. Chromium may play a role in lowering blood glucose levels.

How you live your life may be your business, but think for a moment about how your behaviour can rub off on other people around you. The foods you choose, the exercise you take, even how you talk about your diabetes, can all have an effect on how people in your close family or community choose to live their own lives. For example, you may be a role model for younger people in your social circle, or perhaps people look up to you in some way.

Take the simple example of how you brush your teeth. Think about what is important to you about the way you brush – how do you move the toothbrush, how long do you brush for, what toothpaste do you use, how do you feel when you've done a good job? Even something as simple as the way you brush your teeth says something about you. It shows how important it is for you to get to all the parts of your teeth, and gives an indication of what you are willing to do to look after the health of your teeth and your appearance. All this, believe it or not, is linked to your other behaviours. All our behaviours stem from our identity and every action or behaviour is a reflection of this. So, if you are oozing self-confidence and good health, you will be feeling it on the inside. Choose to show your best side to others so that you can also help them achieve their personal best.

When it comes to people you really care about, it makes sense to encourage them to adopt those healthy habits that you have learnt by managing your own diabetes. Why? Because if you can encourage people to take on the healthy eating and lifestyle patterns recommended for diabetes, you may be able to reduce their risks of developing diabetes or other conditions such as obesity and heart disease. By making simple changes to the habits of the whole family, you could be helping to promote a better quality of life for generations to come…

meal plans

Meal planning enables you to think ahead, think about portion sizes and cooking methods and the combination of foods you plan to eat. Although you can enjoy a range of food, it is important to get the balance right – in fact, this is true whether you have diabetes or not, so planning good choices will be beneficial to the whole family. The recipes in this book have been carefully devised so that they help you meet the dietary recommendations for diabetes, particularly in terms of fat, sugar and carbs. But don't eat lots of dishes at the same time, as that will defeat the purpose. In terms of balance, try to ensure you have the following for each main meal: 1 protein dish (eg. dal, meat, fish, eggs or cheese), 1 vegetable dish (eg. vegetable curry), and 1 carb (eg. roti, rice, potatoes or a combination with smaller portions of each) and serve with a side salad so you get more veg per meal. The plate model on page 18 will give you a good idea of the portion sizes that should fill your plate so you can get balance without having to be too precise.

Diabetes UK guidelines suggest that carbs should make up around half of your daily calorie intake. In this book, which is aimed mainly at people with Type 2 diabetes, we recommend that the total amount of carbs you eat comes to around 275 grams each day. The recipes give you the carb content per serving so you can assess how the carb content of your meal is totting up. Generally, try to make your main meal carbs come to no more than 80 grams, leaving some carbs for your breakfast and snacks. Your fat intake should make up around a third of your daily calories, and in this book, we recommend your fat for the day should come to about 80 grams. We suggest you eat no more than 20 grams of fat for each main meal. The fat will come from added fat in the form of oil, and from fat naturally present in foods like meat and fish. Other nutrients like protein, vitamins and minerals will come together nicely if you keep to the plate model suggestion.

If you are planning a meal combination with a couple of curries, some rice and/or roti, simply look up the analyses and check how you're doing from time to time. Here are some ideas of meals that work well together:

Carrot and tomato soup (page 57)
Tawa vegetables (page 90)
Prawns with baby onions (page 103)
Whole-wheat roti (page 136)
Kachumber salad (page 75)
Piece of fresh fruit

Mixed lentil dal (page 122)
Baby sweetcorn with spinach and garlic (page 85)
Cauliflower and lemon rice (page 141)
Instant vegetable pickle (page 128)
Bowl of strawberries

Slow cooked chicken (page 108)
Vegetable masala (page 85)
Whole-wheat roti (page 136)
Spinach raita (page 133)
Sweet pickle (page 131)
Green pea dessert (page 144)

Chicken in pepper sauce (page 114)
Vegetable pulao (page 93)
Side salad (no oily dressing)
Natural low-fat yogurt and fruit

Quick Tips: If you think you have overdone the carbs, choose a piece of fruit or low fat yogurt for dessert rather than a dessert recipe.

• Remember, you don't need to serve a fancy rice dish – some boiled brown rice is a great choice!

breakfasts

Eating regularly is the basis of your dietary management. When you haven't eaten overnight, your blood glucose is lowered, and you need to break your overnight fast to get your blood glucose levels up again. Breakfast starts your engine and gives you the energy to set you up for the day. It's a chance to have fibre as granary bread or a wholegrain cereal and is a perfect time to start the day with a morning portion of fruit or unsweetened fruit juice. People who eat breakfast tend to be healthier and less overweight, so plenty of reasons to indulge in this chapter!

bajre ki roti with banana stuffing

I believe this millet flatbread can take health foods to new heights. I personally enjoy this for breakfast, especially in the cooler months of the year. Note that whole-wheat flour (atta) is used in the dough because it helps to bind the millet (bajra) dough.

For the stuffing
2 medium-size raw bananas
1/4 teaspoon salt
2 green chillies, chopped
1 teaspoon sugar
1 teaspoon mango powder (amchur)
1 tablespoon chopped fresh coriander leaves

For the bread
65g millet (bajra) flour, sifted
70g whole-wheat flour (atta), sifted plus extra
   for dusting
2 teaspoons roasted sesame seeds

spray olive oil for greasing the tawa

1 First, steam the bananas in their skins for 7–8 minutes. Remove the bananas from the steamer, peel and mash while still hot. Add the salt, green chillies, sugar, mango powder and coriander leaves, and mix until smooth. Divide into four and set aside.

2 For the bread, put the millet and whole-wheat flours in a bowl and mix. Add enough water to make a soft dough. Knead the dough until it is smooth. Divide into four equal-sized balls.

3 Sprinkle some whole-wheat flour on the worktop. Take the first ball and gently, on your floured surface, press it out with your fingers, taking care that the outer edges are thinner than the centre. Spoon a portion of the stuffing in the centre, gather the edges together and roll into a ball again. The stuffing should be totally enclosed in the ball.

4 Press the ball lightly in the roasted sesame seeds, on one side only. Roll it in whole-wheat flour and place on the floured worktop. Gently spread the ball once again to as thin a roti as you can. The sesame seeds will become embedded in the dough. You don't need to use a rolling pin to do this. Repeat the process until all the rotis are made.

5 Heat a lightly greased, non-stick tawa. To cook the flatbreads, simply fry on both sides until lightly golden.

879 kj; 207 kcals; 4.5g protein; 3.4g fat; 0.5g sat fat; 42.2g carbohydrates; 17.4g sugar; 2.6g fibre; 128mg sodium

besan methi frankie (stuffed gram flour roti)

I have replaced some of the whole-wheat flour, which is generally used for frankies, with protein-rich and lower-GI gram flour. A filling and fun breakfast!

90g gram flour (besan)
70g whole-wheat flour (atta), plus extra for dusting
160g fresh fenugreek leaves (methi), chopped
4 green chillies, chopped
1/4 teaspoon ground turmeric
1/4 teaspoon carom seeds (ajwain)
1 tablespoon natural low-fat yogurt
1/2 teaspoon salt
green chutney, as required
1 medium-size onion, chopped

For the stuffing
1 teaspoon olive oil
2 medium-size onions, chopped
2 medium-size tomatoes, seeded and chopped
2 green chillies, chopped
160g beansprouts, blanched
1/4 teaspoon ground turmeric
1/4 teaspoon red chilli powder
1/2 teaspoon chaat masala (see chef's tip, page 136)
1/2 teaspoon salt
1 teaspoon lemon juice
1 tablespoon chopped fresh coriander leaves

1 Mix together the two flours, fenugreek leaves, chillies, turmeric, carom seeds, yogurt and salt. Add enough water to knead into a semi-soft dough. Cover the dough with a damp cloth and rest for about 15 minutes.

2 To make the stuffing, heat the oil in a pan, add the onions and tomatoes and sauté for 2 minutes. Add the chillies and beansprouts and continue to sauté for 30 seconds. Stir in the turmeric, chilli powder, chaat masala, salt, lemon juice and coriander, and sauté for 1 minute. Remove from the heat and set aside.

3 Divide the dough into eight equal-size portions and form into balls. Dust these with a little whole-wheat flour, then roll out into rotis, roughly 15cm in diameter.

4 Heat a non-stick tawa and cook the rotis on both sides, until evenly done.

5 To prepare a frankie, place a roti on a flat work surface and spread a teaspoon of green chutney all over. Spoon some of the stuffing on one side of the roti, sprinkle on some onions, then simply roll up.

6 Prepare the rest of the frankies in the same way, wrapping them in foil as you go to keep them warm and make them easier to handle. Serve immediately.

911 kj; 215 kcals; 12g protein; 3g fat: 0.3g sat fat;
36g carbohydrates; 8.2g sugar; 6.4g fibre; 623mg sodium

brown poha

Flattened rice (poha) is a favourite in many Indian homes as it is nutritious and fast to cook. Brown poha can be found in health-food stores.

250g brown flattened rice (poha)
1 tablespoon olive oil
1 teaspoon black mustard seeds
10–12 curry leaves
2 medium-size onions, chopped
2 green chillies, slit and seeded
30g roasted unsalted peanuts
1/4 teaspoon ground turmeric
1/2 teaspoon salt
40g peas, cooked
1 tablespoon lemon juice
3 tablespoons chopped fresh coriander leaves

1 Soak the brown poha in water for 15–20 minutes. Drain.

2 Heat the oil in a pan. Add the mustard seeds, curry leaves, onions and chillies and sauté for 2 minutes.

3 Stir in the roasted peanuts and turmeric, followed by the soaked poha and salt. Cook for 2–3 minutes.

4 Add the peas and lemon juice and mix again.

5 Garnish with the fresh coriander and serve hot.

1394 kj; 329 kcals; 8g protein; 9g fat; 1.6g sat fat; 58g carbohydrates; 4.4g sugar; 2.8g fibre; 260mg sodium

vegetable upma

Semolina cooked with vegetables is a staple breakfast dish in India. Semolina (rawa or suji) is a great ingredient as it is bulky. It's especially good for breakfast if you know that lunch is going to be late.

1 tablespoon olive oil
1/4 teaspoon black mustard seeds
1 teaspoon split black gram (dhuli urad dal)
6–8 curry leaves
1 small onion, chopped
1 small carrot, diced
3–4 French beans, cut into 1cm pieces
3/4 teaspoon salt
1cm piece root ginger, chopped
2 green chillies, slit
25g peas
1/2 medium-size green pepper, seeded and diced
180g semolina (rawa/suji), roasted
2 tablespoons lemon juice
2 tablespoons chopped fresh coriander leaves

1 Heat the oil in a deep pan. Add the mustard seeds and split black gram. When the seeds begin to splutter, add the curry leaves and onion and sauté until lightly browned.

2 Stir in the diced carrot and French beans, add the salt and cook on a medium heat until the vegetables soften.

3 Add the ginger, green chillies, peas and diced pepper. Mix well, then add 500ml water and let it come to the boil. Cover and cook, on a medium heat, until the vegetables are done.

4 Stir in the semolina, cover and cook on a medium heat until the water has been absorbed and the semolina is tender – about 3–4 minutes. Stir in the lemon juice and coriander leaves, and serve.

877 kj; 207 kcals; 6g protein; 4g fat; 0.6g sat fat; 39g carbohydrates; 2.5g sugar; 2.2g fibre; 379mg sodium

oats with dried fruits

There are many good things about oats: they are fast to cook, good to eat and a fantastic source of fibre. Since you're adding the apricots and prunes, there's no need to add sugar.

85g porridge oats
600ml skimmed milk
4–5 whole almonds, slivered
20g dried apricots, chopped
40g prunes, chopped

1 Put the oats in a pan and roast for 2 minutes. Add the milk and bring to the boil.

2 Stir in the almonds and cook for about 10 minutes, or until the oat mixture becomes thick.

3 Add the apricots and prunes, mix well, and serve hot.

693 kj; 164 kcals; 10g protein; 3g fat; 0.6g sat fat; 27g carbohydrates; 12.9g sugar; 2.8g fibre; 71mg sodium

mooli aur methi ka paratha (radish and fenugreek bread)

Mooli parathas are commonly eaten as a winter breakfast in Punjab. In my friend's kitchen garden in Amritsar they have loads of radishes growing, and the freshness of a mooli just pulled from the ground stuffed into a paratha is unforgettable. I like to add fenugreek too for extra flavour.

1 medium-size radish (mooli), grated
210g whole-wheat flour (atta), plus extra for dusting
1/2 teaspoon ground fenugreek seeds (methi dana)
1/2 teaspoon salt
40g fresh fenugreek leaves (methi), chopped
1/2 teaspoon red chilli powder
pinch of asafoetida
1/2 teaspoon carom seeds (ajwain), crushed
2 green chillies, chopped
2 tablespoons chopped fresh coriander leaves
2 radish (mooli) leaves, chopped
spray olive oil for greasing the tawa

1 Squeeze out any extra juice from the grated mooli. Reserve the juice.

2 Mix together the flour, ground fenugreek and salt. Add the reserved mooli juice, plus extra water if necessary, and knead into a stiff and smooth dough. Cover and leave to rest for 15 minutes.

3 Place the grated mooli, fenugreek leaves, chilli powder, asafoetida, carom seeds, chillies, chopped coriander and mooli leaves in a bowl. Mix well.

4 Divide the dough into four equal portions. Flatten each one with your hand, keeping the edges thinner than the centre. Place a quarter of the mooli filling in the centre, gather the edges together and roll into a ball. Press down slightly, then leave to rest for 5 minutes.

5 After this time, roll out the stuffed dough into a paratha. Place on a preheated tawa and roast on a medium heat until both sides are lightly browned and crisp on the outside. Make the remaining parathas in the same way.

815 kj; 192 kcals; 8g protein; 3g fat; 0.4g sat fat; 36g carbohydrates; 1.8g sugar; 4.8g fibre; 271mg sodium

broken wheat upma

Upma is a wholesome Indian dish made traditionally with semolina, but some regions use cracked wheat. I can't make my mind up about this dish...should I eat it for breakfast or as a light meal, or what? It tastes so good! You can use a pressure cooker for the recipe, but I prefer this slow-cooking method as the wheat swells up more, making it tastier. You could use broccoli instead of carrot and blanched sweetcorn instead of peas – experiment with your favourite combinations of vegetables.

60g natural low-fat yogurt
1 teaspoon salt
1/4 teaspoon black mustard seeds
1 teaspoon split black gram (dhuli urad dal)
10–12 curry leaves
1 medium-size onion, chopped
200g fine broken wheat (lapsi)
2.5cm piece root ginger, chopped
3–4 green chillies, chopped
1 medium-size carrot, diced and blanched
75g peas, blanched (or thawed, if using frozen peas)
1 teaspoon lemon juice
2 tablespoons chopped fresh coriander leaves

1 Put the yogurt, salt and 700ml water in a bowl and whisk until smooth. Set aside.

2 Heat a non-stick pan. Add the mustard seeds and split black gram. When the mustard seeds splutter, add the curry leaves and onion, and cook until lightly browned.

3 Stir in the broken wheat and continue to cook on a medium heat for 2 minutes. Add the chopped ginger and chillies and cook for another 5 minutes, or until fragrant.

4 Mix in the yogurt mixture and bring to the boil. Cook the upma on a low heat, stirring continuously, until all the water is absorbed.

5 Add the carrot and peas, along with lemon juice. Stir gently, adjust the seasoning, and add a little more water if required.

6 Cover and cook on a low heat for another 8–10 minutes.

7 Transfer into a serving bowl and garnish with the coriander.

908 kj; 213 kcals; 8g protein; 1g fat; 0.3g sat fat; 45g carbohydrates; 5g sugar; 1.9g fibre; 513mg sodium

light meals

These quick and easy recipes are ideal for when you're in a rush or you don't fancy a heavy meal – they are perfect for lunch.

What is important is that you get the balance right in terms of carbohydrates, so we have often suggested you have a roti to accompany them. Some of these dishes will also benefit from a serving of salad or a small vegetable dish. We have given you some ideas at the beginning of the recipes to help you get that balance.

chicken aur dal shorba (chicken and dal soup)

Chicken soup is a comfort food in many homes. I like the base of the dal in this recipe because it adds an extra bit of goodness, not to mention an Indian touch. Be careful of what you serve it with, however. This soup is a great low-GI carb dish.

1 teaspoon olive oil
1/2 medium-size onion, chopped
2.5cm piece root ginger, chopped
3 garlic cloves, chopped
2 green chillies, chopped
1/2 teaspoon ground turmeric
1 teaspoon salt
1/2 teaspoon ground cumin
160g split green gram (dhuli moong dal), soaked
1 litre chicken stock
100g boneless chicken, skinned and poached
1 tablespoon lemon juice
2 tablespoons chopped fresh coriander leaves

1 Heat the olive oil in a deep pan. Add the onion and sauté for 1 minute.

2 Add the ginger, garlic and chillies and sauté on a low heat.

3 Add the turmeric, salt, ground cumin and drained dal to the pan, together with the chicken stock. Bring to the boil and cook, on a medium heat, for 10–15 minutes, or until the dal is very soft. Pass through a sieve and return to the pan.

4 Cut the cooked chicken into 5mm dice and add to the strained dal. Bring the mixture to the boil, adding water if necessary to adjust the consistency.

5 Continue to simmer for 2–3 minutes. Add the lemon juice and mix well.

6 Serve the soup piping hot, garnished with the coriander leaves.

1030 kj; 243 kcals; 28g protein; 5g fat; 0.7g sat fat; 22g carbohydrates; 2g sugar; 4.4g fibre; 271mg sodium

gajar aur tamatar shorba (carrot and tomato soup)

Tomato soup tops the list of favourites at home, whereas carrots are often thought of only in terms of gajar halwa (see page 145). So, I thought why not add more nutritional value to the tomato soup by putting in some juicy seasonal carrots? But this soup is not only healthy, it's also delicious. Serve with a roti or a granary roll.

2 medium-size carrots, roughly chopped
8 medium-size tomatoes, roughly chopped
1 medium-size onion, sliced
4 garlic cloves, crushed
1 bay leaf
4–6 black peppercorns
400ml vegetable stock or water
1 teaspoon salt
4–6 fresh mint leaves

1 Pressure-cook the vegetables, bay leaf and peppercorns along with half the vegetable stock or water.

2 Once the vegetables are cooked, let the pressure reduce, then open the lid to allow the mixture to cool.

3 Remove the bay leaf and purée the vegetables to a fine consistency in a blender.

4 Heat the puréed vegetables in a pan, add the remaining vegetable stock or water and add the salt. Add more water if necessary. Simmer for 5 minutes and serve piping hot, garnished with mint leaves.

259 kj; 61 kcals; 2g protein; 1g fat; 0.1g sat fat;
12g carbohydrates; 10.6g sugar; 3.7g fibre; 568mg sodium

palak aur tofu shorba (spinach and tofu soup)

I confess that this is a take-off of the popular spinach and paneer combination. For those who haven't eaten tofu before, it takes some getting used to. Start off with this soup and then gradually add more tofu recipes to your repertoire. Eat with a roti to keep your carbohydrate levels up.

500g spinach leaves
1 teaspoon olive oil
4–5 black peppercorns
1/2 teaspoon cumin seeds
1 medium-size onion, chopped
2.5cm piece root ginger, chopped
2–3 garlic cloves, chopped
1/2 teaspoon salt
1 tablespoon lemon juice
100g tofu, diced

1 Blanch the spinach leaves in plenty of boiling water. Drain and refresh in cold water.

2 Heat the oil in a pan. Add the peppercorns and cumin seeds and fry until they start to change colour. Add the onion and sauté for 2 minutes.

3 Add the ginger and garlic to the pan and sauté until golden.

4 Put the blanched spinach leaves in a blender with 50ml water and blend to a purée. Add this to the pan, plus enough water to give a good consistency. Add the salt and bring the mixture to the boil.

5 Add the lemon juice. Finally, add the tofu to the soup and serve immediately.

287 kj; 68 kcals; 6g protein; 3g fat; 0.4g sat fat;
5g carbohydrates; 3.4g sugar; 3.2g fibre; 423mg sodium

hare moong ka shorba (green gram soup)

We should not underestimate the nutritional value of moong. Eating it in its sprouted form is one way of enjoying it, preparing it as a curry another. In this recipe the moong provides a strong base for an excellent soup. In fact, I like it so much that I have it every week!

150g whole green gram (sabut moong)
1/2 teaspoon salt
1 tablespoon olive oil
1/2 teaspoon cumin seeds
2–3 spring onions, chopped
2.5cm piece root ginger, chopped
3 green chillies, chopped
11/2 tablespoons lemon juice
220g cooked vermicelli

1 Pressure-cook the green gram along with 400ml water and the salt until done. Allow to cool, then grind to a smooth purée. Strain and add up to 1 litre water, stirring to make a thin mixture. Set aside.

2 Heat the oil in a kadai. Add the cumin seeds and, when they begin to change colour, add the spring onions and ginger, and sauté on a medium heat for 30 seconds. Add the chillies and continue to sauté for another 30 seconds.

3 Stir in the gram mixture and bring to the boil. Reduce the heat, add the lemon juice and adjust the seasoning if necessary. Simmer, uncovered, for 5 minutes.

4 Add the vermicelli and simmer for another minute.

5 Pour the soup into serving bowls and serve hot.

842 kj; 199 kcals; 12g protein; 3g fat; 0.4g sat fat;
32g carbohydrates; 1.2g sugar; 3.4g fibre; 253mg sodium

moong ke cheelay (green gram savoury pancakes)

This is a lovely recipe for savoury pancakes, and there's a unique version of coriander chutney to go with them, too. You could eat this with a salad to get your balance of vegetables.

200g whole green gram (sabut moong)
4–5 green chillies, roughly chopped
2.5cm piece root ginger, roughly chopped
4 garlic cloves, roughly chopped
60g natural low-fat yogurt
1/4 teaspoon salt
1/4 teaspoon ground turmeric
1 teaspoon red chilli powder
20g fresh coriander leaves, chopped
spray olive oil
2 medium-size onions, chopped
1 tablespoon chaat masala (see chef's tip page 136)

For the coriander and amla chutney
60g fresh coriander leaves, roughly chopped
140g Indian gooseberries (amla), seeded
3–4 green chillies
1/4 teaspoon salt
1 large slice (30g) of whole-wheat bread

1 Soak the moong in 1 litre water for 6–8 hours. Drain and blend to a smooth batter along with the chillies, ginger, garlic, yogurt and salt. Add water as required to get a batter of dropping consistency.

2 Transfer the batter to a bowl and whisk in the turmeric, chilli powder and fresh coriander. Adjust the seasoning and whisk again to a batter of pouring consistency. Set aside.

3 To prepare the chutney, simply blend all the ingredients until smooth. Transfer to a bowl and set aside.

4 Heat a non-stick flat tawa and spray with a little oil, ready for cooking the pancakes.

5 Pour a ladleful of batter on to the tawa and spread as thinly and evenly as possible, as you would for a dosa. Sprinkle a little of the chopped onion on top, then spray oil around the pancake. Let it cook until the pancake becomes crisp at the edges and turns golden brown. Sprinkle a little chaat masala over it, fold in half, then remove and transfer to a serving plate. Keep warm while you prepare the remaining pancakes in the same way.

6 Serve the pancakes with the coriander and amla chutney.

Chef's note: You can add fresh fenugreek leaves to the batter instead of the coriander leaves if you prefer.

1085 kj; 256 kcals; 17g protein; 3g fat; 0.4g sat fat; 42g carbohydrates; 6.2g sugar; 6.3g fibre; 319mg sodium

dahi idli
(steamed rice cakes in yogurt)

Steamed and soft, this is a comforting and authentic dish. As idlis are quite high in carbohydrate, I suggest you eat them with a salad or a vegetable dish.

220g parboiled rice (ukda chawal)
100g split black gram (dhuli urad dal)
500g natural low-fat yogurt, whisked
2 tablespoons green chutney
2 tablespoons tamarind chutney
1/4 teaspoon red chilli powder
1/4 teaspoon ground cumin
2 tablespoons chopped fresh coriander leaves

1 Wash the rice and then soak in 600ml fresh water for at least 2–3 hours.

2 Wash the dal and then soak in 400ml water for a similar period of time.

3 Drain the rice and grind to a slightly coarse texture. Mix in as much water as required to make a batter of dropping consistency.

4 Drain and grind the dal, then mix to a smooth and spongy batter, again using as much water as required.

5 Mix both the batters together and pour into a large vessel with a lid. Close the lid tightly and then leave the batter to rest, and ferment, in a warm place overnight.

6 The following day, heat sufficient water in a steamer.

7 Place a wet muslin cloth on an idli stand. Pour a spoonful of the fermented batter into each dent. Place the idli stand in the steamer and cook for 8–10 minutes, or until the idlis are done.

8 Place the idlis in a serving bowl and drizzle over the yogurt and chutneys, followed by the chilli powder and ground cumin. Garnish with the chopped coriander leaves and serve.

1433 kj; 337 kcals; 17g protein; 2g fat; 0.8g sat fat; 66g carbohydrates; 11.1g sugar; 2.6g fibre; 225mg sodium

vegetable seekh kebabs

When your guests ask you what is the ingredient that makes these kebabs stand out, you can tell them that it's chhunda (see page 131). You can use mango chutney if chhunda is not available. Serve the kebabs hot with the chutney of your choice. For a tasty lunch (and to keep your carbohydrate levels up) you could serve them in wholemeal pitta bread with salad and natural low-fat yogurt.

1 teaspoon minced root ginger
1 medium-size potato (100g), boiled and mashed
1 medium-size carrot, grated
75g peas, cooked and crushed
5–6 French beans, cooked and finely chopped
1 teaspoon mango powder (amchur)
2 teaspoons chaat masala (see chef's tip, page 136)
3–4 green chillies, chopped
1¹/₂ tablespoons chhunda (see page 131)
3 tablespoons roasted and ground chickpeas (chana)
150g paneer (see chef's tip, page 97), grated
¹/₂ teaspoon salt

1 Heat a non-stick kadai. Add the ginger and cook for 30 seconds. Stir in the mashed potato, carrot, peas and French beans, and roast until the pan gives off a delicious aroma.

2 Add the mango powder, chaat masala, chillies, chhunda, roasted chickpea powder and continue to cook for 2–3 minutes.

3 Stir in the paneer, mixing well, followed by the salt.

4 Divide the mixture into four or eight equal portions. Take each portion and press it around a skewer to form a cylindrical shape.

5 Heat a non-stick tawa and place the skewers on it. Cook on a medium heat, rotating the skewers from time to time so that the kebabs get cooked evenly on all sides, until golden brown.

852 kj; 202 kcals; 11.9g protein; 9.3g fat; 5g sat fat; 18.9g carbohydrates; 6.5g sugar; 1.8g fibre; 875mg sodium

spinach paratha stuffed with paneer

Creating new flavour combinations out of favourite traditional dishes has always been my passion. This recipe strengthens my belief that if you can crack the right combination of ingredients the result is bound to be delicious. This is quite high in carbohydrates and fat so be careful about what you eat during the rest of day.

375g whole-wheat flour (atta), plus extra for dusting
1/2 teaspoon salt
240g spinach, roughly chopped
4 green chillies, chopped
165g natural low-fat yogurt, whisked
180g paneer (see chef's tip, page 97), grated
pinch of asafoetida
2cm piece root ginger, chopped
3 tablespoons chopped fresh coriander leaves
1 1/2 teaspoons carom seeds (ajwain)
1 1/2 teaspoons garam masala powder
7–8 black peppercorns, crushed

1 Sift the whole-wheat flour with the salt, then mix in the spinach, half the green chillies and the yogurt. Knead into a smooth dough, adding water if required. Cover with a damp cloth and set aside for 30 minutes. Divide into eight equal portions.

2 In a deep bowl, mix the paneer, asafoetida, remaining green chillies, ginger, coriander leaves, carom seeds, garam masala and crushed peppercorns. Divide into eight equal portions.

3 On a floured surface, roll out one portion of the dough into a thick disc about 10cm in diameter. Spoon one-eighth of the paneer mixture into the middle, gather the edges and seal. Roll out into a paratha roughly 15cm in diameter. Prepare the other parathas in the same way.

4 Heat a non-stick tawa and cook the parathas until lightly browned on both sides.

1985 kj; 469 kcals; 24.9g protein; 13g fat; 6.6g sat fat; 67.3g carbohydrates; 6.4g sugar; 9.9g fibre; 1017mg

til moongfalli aloo (baby potatoes with sesame and peanuts)

I like to cook these to a crisp. Serve with salad or vegetables and roti.

1 tablespoon olive oil
1 teaspoon cumin seeds
2 green chillies, chopped
2.5cm piece root ginger, chopped
1/2 tablespoon minced garlic
300g baby potatoes, boiled and halved (skin on)
1 tablespoon white sesame seeds
20g unsalted peanuts, coarsely crushed
1 teaspoon ground cumin
1/2 teaspoon red chilli powder
3–4 black peppercorns, crushed
1 tablespoon grated fresh coconut
1 teaspoon garam masala powder
1 teaspoon salt
2 tablespoons chopped fresh coriander leaves

1 Heat the oil in a pan, then add the cumin seeds, green chillies and ginger. When the cumin seeds begin to change colour, add the garlic and sauté for 2 minutes. Stir in the potatoes.

2 Add the sesame seeds, peanuts, ground cumin, chilli powder, crushed peppercorns, coconut and garam masala, and cook for 5 minutes, stirring continuously. Add the salt and transfer to a serving bowl. Garnish with the fresh coriander.

623 kj; 149 kcals; 4g protein; 9g fat; 1.9g sat fat; 15g carbohydrates; 1.5g sugar; 1.6g fibre; 511mg sodium

rajma galouti kababs (red bean kebabs)

I make a point of including these kebabs on my party menu at home. The vegetarian version of the famous, melt-in-the-mouth lamb galouti kebabs can be made variously with yam, peas or spinach, but these, which use red kidney beans, come closest to the original delicacy. Kewra water is an extract that's distilled from pandanus flowers and is used to flavour meats, drinks and desserts in India and Southeast Asia. Some brands of kewra water are artificially flavoured, so check the label. Ideally, the consistency fo the bean paste should be smooth, but it is possible to make the kebabs with a slightly coarse texture as it gives a crisper crust. Serve with a chutney of your choice, a raita and some salad.

200g red kidney beans
8 cashew nuts
1 tablespoon sunflower seeds
1/2 teaspoon caraway seeds
4 green cardamom pods
3 black cardamom pods
2 cloves
2.5cm stick cinnamon
a generous pinch of saffron
1/4 teaspoon kewra water
1 tablespoon olive oil, plus spray oil for greasing
   the pan
1cm piece root ginger, chopped
5 garlic cloves, chopped
3 green chillies, chopped
2 tablespoons grated khoya/mawa
1/2 teaspoon ground white pepper
1 teaspoon salt
1/2 tablespoon lemon juice
1 sprig fresh mint
1 medium-size onion, cut into thin rings

1 Soak the kidney beans in 1 litre water for 8 hours, preferably overnight. Drain, then boil in plenty of fresh water until the beans are soft. Drain and set aside.

2 Dry roast the cashew nuts and sunflower seeds, then grind to a fine paste using a little water.

3 Dry roast the caraway seeds, green and black cardamoms, cloves and cinnamon stick. Cool and grind to a fine powder.

4 Soak the saffron in the kewra water.

5 Heat the oil in a pan, then add the ginger and garlic and sauté for a few seconds. Add the chillies and sauté for 1 minute.

6 Add the cooked kidney beans to the pan and cook for 3–4 minutes. Add the cashew nut paste, stir-fry for 4–5 minutes, then add the khoya, white pepper and salt. Stir-fry for another 4–5 minutes. Remove the pan from the heat and leave the beans to cool.

7 Mash the kidney beans to a smooth paste. (If the paste is not firm, cook it further in a non-stick pan to thicken it up.) Sprinkle on the roasted spices and soaked saffron.

8 Mix in the lemon juice, then divide the mixture into eight equal portions. Press them lightly into patties (tikkis).

9 Heat a non-stick pan and spray it with a little olive oil. Cook the patties until lightly coloured on both sides. Garnish with the mint and onion rings.

957 kj; 227 kcals; 14g protein; 8g fat; 1.4g sat fat; 27g carbohydrates; 3.2g sugar; 8.6g fibre; 510mg sodium

grilled bangda

I took to seafood big time after moving to Mumbai, and ever since I have been gradually increasing my repertoire of fish recipes. This tasty dish is one that I have adapted with healthy eating in mind: while traditional recipes for grilled mackerel use only rice flour, here we have replaced some of the rice flour with lower-GI gram flour. Kokum is commercially sold as a dried rind. It can be bought and kept in air-tight jars for up to a year. Serve the grilled bangda with salad and/or vegetables and a roti.

4 medium-size mackerels (bangda)
1 tablespoon lemon juice
4–5 kokum petals
6–8 garlic cloves
2.5cm piece root ginger
1 teaspoon red chilli powder
1/2 teaspoon ground turmeric
1/4 teaspoon salt
22g gram flour (besan)
35g coarse rice flour
spray olive oil for greasing the pan
1 onion, cut into thin rings

1 Clean the mackerel, inside and out, washing thoroughly. Make four or five 5mm-deep cuts on both sides. Sprinkle on the lemon juice, then set the fish aside for 15 minutes.

2 Soak the kokum petals in 100ml warm water for 15 minutes. Remove the pulp, strain well and set aside.

3 Grind the garlic and ginger to a fine paste. Combine this with the kokum pulp, chilli powder, turmeric, and salt. Use this paste to marinate the mackerels for 30 minutes, preferably in the fridge.

4 Mix the gram flour and rice flour together in a flattish dish. When you are ready to cook the fish, lay them in the flour mixture to coat well on both sides.

5 Spray a little oil on a ridged grill pan and place on the heat. When it is hot, place the coated fish carefully on the pan and grill for 5–6 minutes, turning once, or until the mackerel is cooked on both sides and the surface nicely browned and crisp. If you have to cook the fish in batches, regrease the pan before cooking the next batch. Garnish with the onion rings.

892 kj; 213 kcals; 14g protein; 12g fat; 2.3g sat fat;
13g carbohydrates; 1.8g sugar; 1.2g fibre; 296mg sodium

prawn varuval

Tender, succulent prawns coated in a divine sour dressing and fried to a crisp! It does fire up the appetite... Serve with a kachumber salad and wholemeal pitta bread (see page 75).

5cm piece root ginger
12 garlic cloves
2 tablespoons tamarind pulp
1½ teaspoons ground cumin
2 tablespoons red chilli powder
½ teaspoon ground turmeric
½ teaspoon salt
4 tablespoons rice flour
1½ tablespoons olive oil
32 medium-size prawns, shelled and deveined
1½ tablespoons lemon juice

1 Grind the ginger and garlic to a fine paste and combine with the tamarind pulp, cumin, chilli powder, turmeric, salt and rice flour in a bowl.

2 Blend ½ tablespoon of the olive oil into the mixture, and use this to marinate the prawns for at least 2 hours, preferably in the fridge.

3 Heat the remaining oil in a pan, add the marinated prawns with the marinade and cook for 1 minute on a high heat. Turn the prawns over and cook for another minute. Reduce the heat and cook for a further 2–3 minutes, turning the prawns occasionally to ensure they are done evenly.

4 Remove the prawns from the pan and drain on kitchen paper. Sprinkle with the lemon juice and serve.

947 kj; 224 kcals; 20.8g protein; 6.6g fat; 1.2g sat fat; 21.9g carbohydrates; 6.2g sugar; 0.6g fibre; 526mg sodium

chicken tikka chaat

I love this colourful and flavoursome dish – great for lunch when you have people round. Chaats are typically Indian roadside snacks served in small plates. They are identified by the use of yogurt, chutneys and chaat masala. Serve with roti or sorghum flatbread (see page 139).

1 teaspoon Kashmiri red chilli powder
1 teaspoon minced root ginger
1 teaspoon minced garlic
100g hung natural low-fat yogurt
1/2 teaspoon salt
1/2 teaspoon garam masala powder
2 tablespoons lemon juice
3 teaspoons olive oil
2 boneless chicken breasts (approx. 300g), skinned and cubed
1 small green pepper, seeded and diced
1 small red pepper, seeded and diced
1 small yellow pepper, seeded and diced
1 medium-size onion, sliced
2 green chillies, chopped
1 teaspoon chaat masala (see chef's tip, page 136)
2 tablespoons chopped fresh coriander leaves
1/2 small green mango, chopped (optional)

1 Combine the chilli powder, ginger and garlic pastes, yogurt, salt, garam masala, 1 tablespoon of the lemon juice and 2 teaspoons of the olive oil in a bowl. Add the diced chicken and mix well. Set aside to marinate for 3–4 hours, preferably in the fridge.

2 Preheat the oven to 200ºC/400ºF/gas mark 6. Alternatively, preheat a tandoor.

3 Thread the chicken pieces on to skewers and cook in the preheated oven (or a moderately hot tandoor), for 10–12 minutes, or until almost done. Baste the chicken with the remaining oil and cook for another 4 minutes. Set aside to cool. Remove the chicken from the skewers.

4 In a large bowl, combine the chicken tikkas with the diced peppers, onion, chillies, chaat masala, half the coriander, the remaining lemon juice and the mango (if using), and toss well.

5 Transfer to a serving dish and serve garnished with the remaining coriander.

703 kj; 167 kcals; 22g protein; 4g fat; 1g sat fat; 10g carbohydrates; 8g sugar; 1.6g fibre; 348mg sodium

tofu chana dal

This is one of my home recipes which I have modified for this book. We usually make it with pieces of deep-fried paneer, so this version is definitely healthier! Eat with a raita of your choice.

150g split Bengal gram (chana dal)
1 tablespoon olive oil, plus spray oil for greasing
 the pan
200g tofu, cut into small cubes
1/2 teaspoon black mustard seeds
10–12 curry leaves
2 pinches of asafoetida
1/2 teaspoon salt
1/4 teaspoon ground turmeric
2 1/2 tablespoons lemon juice
20g fresh mint leaves, chopped

1 Soak the chana dal in 400ml water for 3–4 hours.

2 Spray olive oil on a heated frying pan and toss the tofu until brown specks form on it. Remove and set aside.

3 Heat the olive oil in a pan and add the mustard seeds and curry leaves. As the seeds begin to splutter, stir in the asafoetida. Add the drained chana dal and salt and sauté for 2 minutes.

4 Stir in the turmeric and 100ml water, cover, and cook for 10–12 minutes, or until the chana dal is done.

5 Add the tofu, lemon juice and mint leaves. Cook for 30 seconds, then remove from the heat.

798 kj; 189 kcals; 12.6g protein; 7.1g fat; 0.7g sat fat;
19.9g carbohydrates; 1.2g sugar; 0.3g fibre; 268mg sodium

grilled salt-and-pepper tofu

This dish is one of the quickest to make and one of the lightest to eat. It is very low in carbs and calories, so perfect for a light snack. Or you could roll the tofu in a roti with some salad and chutney for a delicious portable lunch.

1 tablespoon olive oil
2 spring onions, chopped, plus the finely chopped
 green parts of 4–6 spring onions
5cm piece root ginger, chopped
6 garlic cloves, chopped
5cm stalk celery, chopped
2 green chillies, sliced
200g tofu, cut into 2cm cubes
1/8 teaspoon salt
7–8 black peppercorns, crushed
1 tablespoon lemon juice

1 Heat the oil in a pan. Add the spring onions, ginger and garlic, and sauté for 2 minutes. Add the celery and green chillies and sauté for 30 seconds.

2 Stir in the tofu, salt and crushed peppercorns and sauté until the tofu gets some brown flecks.

3 Add the spring onion greens and sauté for 1 minute.

4 Add the lemon juice, toss and serve.

289 kj; 69 kcals; 4g protein; 5g fat; 0.7g sat fat;
2g carbohydrates; 0.7g sugar; 0.6g fibre; 67mg sodium

salads

These wonderful dishes add valuable nutrients and fibre to any meal. Most of the salads are low in carbohydrates and calories, so choose them often as accompaniments to light meals and main dishes.

Salads with carbohydrates, like the warm potato salad and the bulgur wheat salad, can still be enjoyed, but make sure you don't eat too many other carbohydrates (like rice and roti) at the same meal.

kachumber salad (vegetable salad)

This is a great everyday salad. Apart from a certain amount of chopping, it is quick and easy to make. I have already taught our elder daughter to make this one, especially if there is a rajma chawal lunch planned at home. As this salad is so low in calories, fat and carbohydrates but full of nutrients, it is the perfect partner for any of the light meals and main dishes in this book. Get into the habit of having this sort of salad on the table at mealtimes.

1 medium-size tomato, seeded and diced
1 medium-size cucumber, seeded and diced
1 medium-size green pepper, seeded and diced
1/2 medium-size white radish, diced
1 medium-size carrot, diced
1 medium-size onion, chopped
2 green chillies, chopped
2 tablespoons chopped fresh coriander leaves
1 tablespoon lemon juice
1/2 teaspoon salt

1 Simply mix all the ingredients in a bowl and toss well. Serve at room temperature.

128 kj; 30 kcals; 1g protein; 0g fat; 0g sat fat;
6g carbohydrates; 5.1g sugar; 1.7g fibre; 259mg sodium

khamang kakdi (cucumber salad)

This is a bowlful of crunchy goodness that is best made just minutes before eating. I first ate it at the home of a Maharashtrian friend of mine. Due to the peanuts, this is quite high in fat so don't eat it with a high-in-fat meat main dish. Traditionally, coconut is added in this salad but I have not used it here to decrease the fat content.

3 medium-size cucumbers, seeded and chopped
2 green chillies, finely chopped
100g unsalted peanuts, roasted, peeled and
   coarsely ground
1 tablespoon lemon juice
1 teaspoon sugar
1 teaspoon olive oil
1/2 teaspoon black mustard seeds
1/4 teaspoon cumin seeds
1/2 teaspoon salt
30g fresh coriander leaves, chopped

1 Mix the chopped cucumber with the chillies, ground peanuts, lemon juice and sugar.

2 Heat the olive oil in a small pan, add the mustard seeds and let them splutter. Add the cumin seeds to the pan and stir-fry briefly.

3 Stir the fried seeds into the cucumber mixture, add the salt and garnish with the coriander leaves. Serve immediately.

779 kj; 186 kcals; 7.9g protein; 14.2g fat; 2.6g sat fat;
7.1g carbohydrates; 4.3g sugar; 1.9g fibre; 252mg sodium

peppery corn and tomato salad

I love this particular medley for its sweet tang – try it, and you may just love it too!

300g sweetcorn kernels
1 medium-size yellow pepper, seeded and diced
2 medium-size green peppers, seeded and diced
3 medium-size tomatoes, seeded and diced
2 slices of pineapple (approx. 100g), diced
2 tablespoons lemon juice
15–20 black peppercorns, crushed
2 green chillies, chopped
15g fresh mint leaves, chopped

1 Boil the sweetcorn in water until soft. Drain thoroughly and cool.

2 In a bowl, combine the cooled sweetcorn with the diced peppers, tomatoes and pineapple. Add the lemon juice, crushed black peppercorns, chillies and mint, and give it a good stir.

3 Arrange the salad in a serving dish and chill in the fridge before serving.

475 kj; 112 kcals; 4g protein; 2g fat; 0.2g sat fat;
21g carbohydrates; 9g sugar; 3.5g fibre; 11mg sodium

phalon ka kachumber (mixed fruit salad)

Fruit and vegetables can taste wonderful when combined in salads, and this kachumber is particularly light and healthy. It is quite high in carbohydrates, so be aware when you are choosing rice or roti accompaniments for the same meal.

2 medium-size apples
2 tablespoons lemon juice
2 medium-size oranges
1 medium-size cucumber
12–15 seedless green grapes, halved
12–15 seedless black grapes, halved
2 medium-size tomatoes, seeded and cut into strips
1 medium-size green pepper, seeded and cut into strips
2 spring onions, thinly sliced
30g fresh coriander leaves, chopped
15g fresh mint leaves, chopped
2 green chillies, chopped
1 teaspoon chaat masala (see chef's tip, page 136)
1/2 teaspoon salt

1 Core the apples, cut in half and then slice thinly. Sprinkle 1 tablespoon of the lemon juice over the apples immediately to prevent discolouration.

2 Peel the oranges and separate into segments. Cut each segment in half, removing any pips. Cut the cucumber in half lengthways and slice thinly.

4 Prepare the remaining fruit and vegetables as required and place with the other salad ingredients in a bowl.

5 For the dressing, simply combine the chopped coriander and mint, chillies, chaat masala, salt and remaining lemon juice. Toss the salad in the dressing and serve chilled.

384 kj; 90 kcals; 3g protein; 1g fat; 0g sat fat;
20g carbohydrates; 18.9g sugar; 3.4g fibre; 261mg sodium

lapsi aur phal salad (bulgur wheat and fruit salad)

South Asians use cracked wheat to make milk-based puddings like kheer and also halwas called lapsi. It is also cooked with dals and vegetables to make a porridge and khichdi. There are different grades of cracked wheat available ranging from fine to coarse. Broken wheat is a more common name. This is a colourful dish that could be eaten for lunch or as the perfect carbohydrate and salad two-in-one to accompany a vegetable or meat main dish.

200g bulgur wheat (lapsi)
2 medium-size red peppers
1 medium-size yellow pepper
1 medium-size onion, sliced
4 garlic cloves, thinly sliced
2 medium-size tomatoes, seeded and diced
1 tablespoon chopped fresh parsley
1/2 teaspoon salt
ground white pepper to taste
pinch of sugar
1 tablespoon lemon juice
1 medium-size apple, diced
4 tablespoons finely chopped fresh mint leaves
a few leaves of Iceberg lettuce
1 tablespoon olive oil

1 Soak the cracked wheat in water for 15 minutes, then strain.

2 Push each pepper on to a fork and, one at a time, roast directly on a flame. (If you prefer, you can char the peppers under the grill or roast them in the oven.)

3 Put the soaked wheat into a salad bowl, and stir in the onion and garlic.

4 Run water on the charred peppers and then remove the burnt skin. Cut the flesh into small pieces and add to the salad bowl.

5 Stir in the tomatoes and parsley, then add the salt, white pepper and sugar and mix. Add the lemon juice, apple and mint leaves.

6 Tear up the Iceberg lettuce and add. Toss well.

7 Add the olive oil, toss again and serve immediately.

800 kj; 189 kcals; 5g protein; 4g fat; 0.5g sat fat; 36g carbohydrates; 12.5g sugar; 3.1g fibre; 258mg sodium

kosumali
(mixed sprout and vegetable salad)

A salad means a medley of vegetables, right? So if you add some pulses to it, does the appeal increase? It certainly does in this case. Kosumali is so vividly coloured and textured that it is brilliant for children as well as adults. Serve with a curry to get your vegetable and fibre levels up.

100g split green gram (dhuli moong dal)
80g beansprouts (moong sprouts)
2 medium-size carrots, grated
1 medium-size cucumber, seeded and chopped
2 green chillies, chopped
1 medium-size mango, chopped
2 tablespoons chopped fresh coriander leaves
1 tablespoon lemon juice
1/2 teaspoon salt
2 teaspoons olive oil
1 teaspoon black mustard seeds
8–10 curry leaves
1 tablespoon grated fresh coconut

1 Soak the dal in 200ml water for 30 minutes. Drain and place in a pan. Add another 200ml water and cook until the dal is just done. Drain again and set aside to cool.

2 Boil the beansprouts until just cooked. Drain and set aside.

3 In a large bowl, mix together the dal and beansprouts, carrots, cucumber, chillies, mango and chopped coriander. Add the lemon juice and salt and mix well.

4 Heat the oil in a pan. Add the mustard seeds, roast until they splutter, and then add the curry leaves. Add this tempering to the dal mixture and give it a good stir.

5 Garnish with the grated coconut and serve at room temperature.

688 kj; 162 kcals; 9g protein; 3g fat; 1g sat fat; 26g carbohydrates; 13.6g sugar; 5.6g fibre; 263mg sodium

warm potato salad

This salad is different because the vegetables are marinated and then roasted like tandoori preparations. As it's higher in carbohydrates than most salads, cut down on your rice and roti accompaniments.

135g hung natural low-fat yogurt
1 tablespoon ginger-garlic-green chilli paste
  (see chef's tip)
1/2 teaspoon salt
1/2 teaspoon ground black pepper
16 baby potatoes (300–350g), parboiled
16 baby onions
1 medium-size green pepper
1 medium-size red pepper
1 medium-size yellow pepper
2 teaspoons olive oil
2 tablespoons green chutney
1 tablespoon lemon juice
1/2 teaspoon chaat masala (see chef's tip, page 136)

1 Mix together the hung yogurt, ginger-garlic-chilli paste, salt and black pepper and use to marinate the potatoes and onions for 15 minutes.

2 Thread the peppers on to skewers and hold them over a gas flame to roast, turning them so that they cook evenly all over and the skin gets almost charred. Or you can char them under the grill. Let the peppers cool slightly, then remove the skin and roughly chop the flesh.

3 Thread the marinated potatoes and onions on to skewers. Heat a tawa, add the oil, then lay on the skewers. Cook on a medium heat, rotating the skewers so that the potatoes and onions turn an even light brown.

4 Combine the chopped peppers, potatoes and onions in a bowl. Add the chutney, lemon juice and chaat masala, and toss well. Serve warm.

606 kj; 143 kcals; 7g protein; 3g fat; 0.7g sat fat;
23g carbohydrates; 10.8g sugar; 2.8g fibre; 393mg sodium

Chef's tip: To make ginger-garlic-green chilli paste, pound 50g root ginger, 2 garlic cloves and 100g chopped green chillies together with a pinch of salt until a smooth paste is formed. Store in a clean glass jar in the fridge. It keeps well for a month if frozen in ziplock bags.

vegetables

Vegetables are an essential part of your daily menu. Choose them often as either side dishes or main meals. These tasty recipes will add colour and crunch (if you don't overcook your vegetables!) to any dining table. Vegetables also help to slow down the rise in blood glucose after a meal, so they are particularly important for people with diabetes.

Note that some of these dishes may be a little high in salt for a side dish, so remember not to add any salt at the table.

If you are a vegetarian or don't like to eat too much meat/fish we have got some dishes with paneer, tofu and pulses to give you a valuable portion of protein. Remember that you must eat some protein at every meal.

tindora nu shaak (stir-fried gherkins)

Tindora (or tindli) are ivy gourds, gherkin-like vegetables that are delicious tossed with some spices, especially when juicy, fresh and tender. This is a brilliant vegetable accompaniment to any main dish.

1 tablespoon olive oil
1/4 teaspoon black mustard seeds
pinch of asafoetida
300g gherkins (tindora/tindli), thinly sliced
1 teaspoon ground coriander
1 teaspoon ground cumin
1/4 teaspoon ground turmeric
1/2 teaspoon salt

1 Heat the oil in a kadai. Add the mustard seeds and asafoetida. When the seeds begin to splutter, add the sliced gherkins and sauté on a low heat for 5–7 minutes.

2 Add all the masala spices and the salt and cook on a high heat for 2–3 minutes.

3 Remove from the heat when crisp.

186 kj; 45 kcals; 1g protein; 3g fat; 0.4g sat fat;
3g carbohydrates; 1.2g sugar; 0.6g fibre; 256mg sodium

punjabi bhindi (stir-fried okra)

Visit a Punjabi home in the summer and you will not need to guess what's cooking! Okra or lady's fingers (bhindi) cooked in this simple manner add grace to the lunch table. And they are delicious with any curry and roti.

500g okra (bhindi)
1 tablespoon olive oil
1/2 teaspoon cumin seeds
3 large onions, thickly sliced
1 green chilli, slit
1/2 teaspoon red chilli powder
1 teaspoon ground coriander
1/4 teaspoon ground turmeric
1/2 teaspoon salt
1/2 teaspoon mango powder (amchur)

1 Trim the heads and tails of the okra, then cut into 5cm-long pieces. Slit each horizontally without cutting them into two.

2 Heat the oil in a kadai and add the cumin seeds. Sauté briefly, then add the onions and green chilli and sauté for 30 seconds.

3 Add the okra, then sprinkle on the chilli powder, coriander and turmeric. Mix well, cover, and cook over a low heat for 5–7 minutes, stirring occasionally. Add the salt and mango powder and cook for a further 2 minutes.

492 kj; 117 kcals; 5g protein; 4g fat; 0.5g sat fat;
16g carbohydrates; 10.7g sugar; 5.8g fibre; 265mg sodium

baby sweetcorn and spinach with garlic

If you like garlic this simple recipe is for you. It can be ready in a jiffy, though the taste lingers. As it's very low in calories and carbs, you could have with rice and dal.

1 tablespoon olive oil
5–6 garlic cloves, sliced
1/4 teaspoon asafoetida
2 green chillies, chopped
375g baby sweetcorn, cut into small pieces
125g spinach, blanched and puréed
1 teaspoon garam masala powder
1/2 teaspoon salt
1/2 tablespoon lemon juice
2 tablespoons chopped fresh coriander leaves

1 Heat the oil in a kadai, add the garlic and sauté until golden brown. Add the asafoetida and chillies and sauté for 10 seconds.

2 Add the baby sweetcorn, sauté for 2 minutes, then add the spinach purée, garam masala and salt. Sauté for a further 2 minutes.

3 Sprinkle on the lemon juice and garnish with the coriander leaves.

268 kj; 64 kcals; 4g protein; 4g fat; 0.4g sat fat; 4g carbohydrates; 2.4g sugar; 2.7g fibre; 347mg sodium

vegetable masala

This is a dish for people on a mission to eat more vegetables! There is something appealing about cooking vegetables in a spicy masala, particularly when you know that there is endless scope to adapt the masala to suit your own tastes. Serve with whole-wheat rotis.

2 teaspoons olive oil
1 medium-size onion, sliced
500g cauliflower, broken into florets
25g peas
1 medium-size carrot, diced
5–6 French beans, chopped
1 teaspoon salt
1/2 tablespoon tamarind pulp
2 tablespoons chopped fresh coriander leaves

For the masala
2 tablespoons grated fresh coconut
1/2 tablespoon ground coriander
1/2 tablespoon red chilli powder
1/2 tablespoon garam masala powder
1/4 teaspoon ground turmeric
1 teaspoon minced ginger and garlic

1 Grind all the ingredients for the masala, adding water as required, into a fine paste.

2 Heat the oil in a non-stick kadai and sauté the onion on a medium heat until golden.

3 Stir in all the vegetables one by one. Add the salt and 200ml water and bring to the boil. Lower the heat, cover, and cook until the vegetables are tender.

4 Stir in the tamarind pulp and masala paste, then simmer for 2 minutes. Garnish with the coriander leaves.

486 kj; 116 kcals; 6g protein; 6g fat; 1.9g sat fat; 11g carbohydrates; 6.9g sugar; 3.9g fibre; 530mg sodium

bharwan karele (stuffed bitter gourds)

Bitter gourds are considered to be among the most nutritious gourds. There is reason to suggest that karele can keep lower blood glucose levels (page 43). I have learnt the knack of converting karela-haters into karela-lovers. This recipe helps 100 per cent! In fact, it's so attractive that I dare to serve it at dinner parties. You could have this as a main meal with a roti or some rice if you wish.

8 medium-size bitter gourds (karela), approx. 700g
90g gram flour (besan)
2 medium-size onions, chopped
2 tablespoons chopped fresh coriander leaves
1 teaspoon salt
1 teaspoon red chilli powder
1/4 teaspoon garam masala powder
1 teaspoon carom seeds (ajwain)
2 teaspoons fennel seeds
1 tablespoon olive oil
2 teaspoons minced ginger
1 tablespoon minced garlic
1 teaspoon ground coriander
1 teaspoon ground cumin
1/2 teaspoon ground turmeric
2 teaspoons tamarind pulp

1 Scrape the bitter gourds, then make a slit on one side of each one and remove the seeds. Rub salt inside and out and set aside for an hour. Then rinse under running water two or three times. Set aside.

2 To prepare the stuffing, dry roast the gram flour in a non-stick pan on a low heat until fragrant. Remove from the heat, transfer to a plate and allow to cool.

3 In a bowl, combine the cooled gram flour with half the onions, the coriander leaves, salt, half the red chilli powder, the garam masala, carom seeds and fennel seeds, and mix well.

4 Stuff this masala mixture into the bitter gourds.

5 Heat the oil in a pan, add the remaining onions and sauté until light golden brown. Add the minced ginger and garlic and sauté for 2 minutes.

6 Next, add the remaining chilli powder, the ground coriander, cumin and turmeric, and mix well. Sauté the masala until fragrant.

7 Add the stuffed bitter gourds to the pan, along with 100ml water. Cover and cook on a high heat for 3–4 minutes. Then reduce the heat and cook for 10–12 minutes, stirring gently at regular intervals.

8 Add the tamarind pulp and mix well. Cover once again and cook for another 10–15 minutes, until the bitter gourds are properly cooked.

696 kj; 165 kcals; 9g protein; 6g fat; 0.6g sat fat; 20g carbohydrates; 4.1g sugar; 7.5g fibre; 523mg sodium

karele andhra style

I have yet to see such a marvellous avatar of bitter gourds. And it takes only a little oil to cook them so brilliantly. These gourds are seldom mixed with other vegetables because of their strong bitter taste, but you can eat them with a curry and some rice as a great vegetable accompaniment.

4–5 medium-size bitter gourds (karela)
2.5cm piece root ginger
5 garlic cloves
4 dried red chillies
1 tablespoon coriander seeds
1 teaspoon cumin seeds
1 teaspoon sesame seeds
1½ teaspoons olive oil
2 medium-size onions, chopped
4 tablespoons tomato purée
1 tablespoon grated jaggery
2 tablespoons tamarind pulp
1 teaspoon salt

1 Scrape the bitter gourds and and then cut them in half lengthways. Remove the seeds and slice thinly. Sprinkle over some salt and set aside for 10–15 minutes. Then wash the gourds with plenty of water, drain and squeeze out any excess water.

2 Grind the ginger and garlic together to form a fine paste.

3 Heat a tawa, then roast the chillies and coriander, cumin and sesame seeds on a medium heat until light brown, stirring continuously. Cool the mixture and then grind to a fine powder.

4 Heat the oil in a non-stick pan. Add the sliced gourds and stir-fry for 4–5 minutes, until slightly browned. Add the chopped onions and stir-fry for 3–4 minutes. Add the ginger-garlic paste, stir-fry for 1–2 minutes, then add the tomato purée and cook for a further few minutes.

5 Stir in the ground spices, grated jaggery, tamarind pulp and salt, and mix well. Add 200ml water and bring to the boil. Then reduce the heat to medium, cover and simmer for 5 minutes.

448 kj; 106 kcals; 4g protein; 3g fat; 0.3g sat fat; 17g carbohydrates; 13.2g sugar; 3.5g fibre; 241mg sodium

chorchori
(bengali mixed vegetables)

1 tablespoon mustard oil
1½ teaspoons panch phoron (see chef's tip)
½ teaspoon red chilli powder
125g cauliflower, broken into small florets
2 medium-size potatoes (200g), diced
1 medium-size sweet potato (100g), diced
100g pumpkin, diced
1 medium-size long brinjal, diced
6–8 French beans, cut into 1cm pieces
6–8 spinach leaves, shredded
¼ teaspoon ground turmeric
2 green chillies, slit
½ teaspoon sugar
1 teaspoon salt

1 Heat the oil in a non-stick pan until it reaches smoking point. Remove from the heat, cool and heat the oil again on a medium heat.

2 Add the panch phoron and, when it begins to crackle, add the chilli powder, stirring briefly. Stir in the prepared vegetables, followed by the turmeric, chillies, sugar and salt. Reduce the heat, cover and cook for 8–10 minutes, stirring occasionally or until the potatoes are cooked.

3 Uncover and stir-fry for 1 minute and or until the chorchori is dry.

Chef's tip: Panch phoron, also known as Bengali five spice, can be bought ready made, but it is easy to make at home. Simply mix together equal quantities of black mustard seeds, cumin seeds, fenugreek seeds, fennel seeds and onion seeds.

532 kj; 126 kcals; 4g protein; 4g fat; 0.5g sat fat; 19g carbohydrates; 5.5g sugar; 4g fibre; 538mg sodium

This delectable mix of vegetables comes straight from Bengal. The story goes that in many Bengali households, shopping for fresh vegetables was the duty of the man of the house; and this was done once a week on his day off from work. By the end of the week, the lady of the house was left with bits of all sorts of vegetables – hence this nutritious medley! Eat with a small amount of rice, dal and natural low-fat yogurt.

khumb hara dhania (mushrooms with fresh coriander)

Mushrooms have a wonderful ability to absorb flavours. This recipe uses mild spices but lots of fresh coriander to coat the mushrooms with a succulent masala. Serve simply with steamed brown rice or with whole-wheat rotis.

600g button mushrooms, trimmed
1 tablespoon olive oil
5 green cardamom pods
1 black cardamom pod
5 cloves
2.5cm stick cinnamon
1 bay leaf
pinch of ground mace
175g boiled onion paste (see chef's tip)
4 teaspoons minced ginger
4 teaspoons minced garlic
4 green chillies, chopped
1 teaspoon red chilli powder
1/2 teaspoon ground coriander
375g natural low-fat yogurt, whisked
1/2 teaspoon salt
3 tablespoons cashew nut paste
25g fresh coriander leaves, chopped
3.5cm piece root ginger, cut into thin strips

1 Blanch the mushrooms in hot water for 2 minutes. Drain and set aside.

2 Heat the oil in a kadai. Add the cardamom pods, cloves, cinnamon, bay leaf and mace and sauté over a medium heat until fragrant.

3 Add the onion paste and sauté for 2–3 minutes. Stir in the minced ginger and garlic and continue to sauté until the oil surfaces. Add the chillies and sauté for 30 seconds more, before adding the chilli powder and ground coriander. Stir for another 30 seconds.

4 Remove the pan from the heat and stir in the yogurt and salt. Mix well, then return the pan to the heat. Add 150ml water and let it come to the boil. Reduce the heat and simmer until the fat rises to the surface.

5 Stir in the cashew nut paste and simmer for 2–3 minutes.

6 Add the mushrooms and three-quarters of the chopped coriander and simmer for 2–3 minutes.

7 Transfer the mushrooms to a serving dish and garnish with the remaining coriander and the ginger strips.

Chef's tip: For the onion paste, peel and roughly chop 4–5 medium-size onions. Put them in a pan, add 1 bay leaf, 1 black cardamom pod and 50ml water. Bring to the boil, simmer until the onions are transparent and the liquid has evaporated. Cool, then discard the bay leaf and cardamom. Transfer the onions to a blender and process to a fine purée.

783 kj; 187 kcals; 10.8g protein; 10.5g fat; 1.8g sat fat; 13.1g carbohydrates; 8.2g sugar; 2.5g fibre; 343mg sodium

tawa vegetables
(griddle fried vegetables)

This medley of vegetables in a spicy tomato sauce is a popular dish at Indian weddings. As this dish requires a little more oil than usual, be careful of the fat content in accompanying dishes.

2 bitter gourds (karela), peeled, seeded and
  cut into batons
4 medium-size snake gourds (parwar), halved
8 gherkins (tindora/tindli), halved
2 tablespoons olive oil
4 small aubergines (brinjal), each cut into
  four lengthways
8 okra (bhindi), each cut into four lengthways
8 baby potatoes (180g), boiled
8 button or pearl onions
6 button mushrooms, quartered
3 medium-size onions, chopped
3.5cm piece root ginger, chopped
3–4 green chillies, seeded and chopped
1/2 teaspoon red chilli powder
1 teaspoon ground coriander
6 medium-size tomatoes, puréed
3/4 teaspoon salt
2 teaspoons mango powder (amchur)
20g fresh coriander leaves, chopped

1 Steam the bitter gourds, snake gourds and gherkins. Set aside.

2 Heat 1 tablespoon of the oil in a non-stick kadai. Add the aubergines and okra and toss. Cook on a medium heat for 2 minutes.

3 Add the potatoes and continue to cook for 2 minutes. Add the button onions and mushrooms and cook for a further 2 minutes. Mix with the gourds and gherkins.

4 Heat the remaining oil in another kadai. Add the chopped onions and ginger and sauté for 1 minute.

5 Stir in the green chillies, chilli powder, ground coriander, puréed tomatoes, salt and mango powder. Cook until the oil surfaces.

6 Heat a griddle. Place half the cooked vegetables on the griddle, along with half the prepared curry. Stir and cook until the vegetables are well coated. Repeat the process with the remaining vegetables and curry. (You can sauté the vegetables in individual portions if you prefer.) Garnish with the coriander leaves.

767 kj; 182 kcals; 6g protein; 8g fat; 0.9g sat fat;
24g carbohydrates; 13.4g sugar; 8g fibre; 409mg sodium

pumpkin foogath

I love having some fast-to-cook recipes to hand, and this stir-fry is one of them. From chopping board to table I can assure you that it takes less than 15 minutes. This wipes away all excuses of being 'too tired to cook'! It also goes to show that fast food doesn't have to be unhealthy. Traditionally in India pumpkin is chopped finely, but as modern cooks have less time it is faster to cube it and cook it! Serve with your favourite curry and some rice or a roti.

1 tablespoon olive oil
1/4 teaspoon black mustard seeds
10–12 curry leaves
2 medium-size onions, chopped
3 green chillies, chopped
700g red pumpkin, cubed
1/2 teaspoon salt
1 tablespoon grated fresh coconut
1 tablespoon lemon juice

1 Heat the oil in a kadai and add the mustard seeds and curry leaves. When the mustard seeds start to splutter, add the onions and chillies. Stir on a high heat for 1 minute.

2 Add the diced red pumpkin and salt. Cook, covered, on a low heat for 5–7 minutes, or until the pumpkin is cooked.

3 Add the grated coconut and lemon juice and mix well.

325 kj; 78 kcals; 2g protein; 4g fat; 1.2g sat fat;
8g carbohydrates; 6g sugar; 2.6g fibre; 248mg sodium

vegetable pulao

I find this an appropriate way to dress up simple brown rice. Our cook at home has mastered the art of cooking brown rice to perfection and this recipe is, as you'd expect, faultless. Serve it with a curry for four or have as a main meal for two people.

190g brown basmati rice
2 teaspoons olive oil
1 bay leaf
2–3 cloves
1 teaspoon cumin seeds
2.5cm stick cinnamon
1/2 teaspoon salt
2 medium-size carrots, diced
10–12 French beans, cut into 1cm pieces
125g cauliflower, broken into small florets
6–7 button mushrooms, halved (optional)
2 green chillies, slit
75g peas, blanched (or thawed if you use frozen)
30g chickpeas (kabuli chana), soaked and cooked
2 tablespoons chopped fresh coriander leaves

1 Soak the brown rice in 1 litre water for 2 hours. Drain and set aside.

2 Heat a deep non-stick pan. Add the oil, followed by the bay leaf, cloves, cumin seeds and cinnamon, and sauté for a few seconds or until the spices are fragrant.

3 Stir in the drained rice and salt and roast for 1–2 minutes. Add 700ml water, bring to the boil, then add the carrots, French beans, cauliflower, mushrooms and chillies. Return to the boil, reduce the heat, cover and cook for 35 minutes.

4 Add the peas and chickpeas and mix gently. Cover and cook until the chickpeas are tender. Garnish with the coriander leaves.

1008 kj; 238 kcals; 7g protein; 4g fat; 0.7g sat fat;
47g carbohydrates; 5g sugar; 3.8g fibre; 262mg sodium

sarson ka saag (mustard greens)

The classic pairing of peppery mustard greens (sarson ka saag) and hand-rolled cornbread (makki ki roti) comes into its own on chilly winter days in North India. If you can't get hold of bathua, a popular winter leaf in India, simply replace with more spinach. Serve with makki ki roti.

2 tablespoons cornmeal (makai ka atta)
1 tablespoon olive oil
2 medium-size onions, chopped
5cm piece root ginger, chopped
6–8 garlic cloves, chopped
4–6 green chillies, chopped
1 teaspoon red chilli powder
1kg mustard greens (sarson ka saag), roughly chopped
125g spinach, roughly chopped
45g bathua leaves (optional), roughly chopped
1/2 teaspoon salt

1 Blend the cornmeal to a paste with 100ml water.

2 Heat the oil in a pan, add the onions and sauté for 2–3 minutes, or until translucent.

3 Add the ginger, garlic and chillies and stir-fry briefly. Stir in the chilli powder and mustard, spinach and bathua leaves. Add 100ml water and cook on a medium heat for 10 minutes, stirring occasionally.

4 Stir in the blended cornmeal and cook for a further 5–6 minutes, stirring continuously.

5 Cool the mixture slightly and blend to a coarse paste. Reheat, stir well and serve.

607 kj; 144 kcals; 8g protein; 4g fat; 0.5g sat fat;
20g carbohydrates; 5.4g sugar; 1g fibre; 323mg sodium

soya bean khichdi

Soya beans have a low glycaemic index. In fact, all beans have a low glycaemic index, but soya beans particularly so. Try to include them in your diet for their excellent health benefits. A healthy meal in one!

100g soya beans, soaked overnight in water
  and drained
145g brown basmati rice, soaked in water
  and drained
3 medium-size tomatoes, chopped
3 green chillies, slit
1 teaspoon olive oil
1/2 teaspoon cumin seeds
2 medium-size onions, sliced
1 teaspoon minced ginger and garlic
1/2 teaspoon ground turmeric
60g natural low-fat yogurt, plus extra to serve
1/2 teaspoon salt
75g peas, cooked
10–12 French beans, cut into 1cm pieces and boiled
15g fresh coriander leaves, chopped
15g fresh mint leaves, chopped

1 Bring 1 litre water to the boil in a deep pan. Add the drained soya beans and rice, along with the tomatoes and green chillies. Cook until both the rice and beans are done – about 35–40 minutes.

2 Heat the oil in a non-stick pan and add the cumin seeds. When the seeds begin to change colour, add the onion and ginger-garlic paste and sauté until the onion is golden.

3 Stir in the turmeric, yogurt, salt, peas and French beans, mixing well, followed by the cooked rice and beans. Add 200ml water and the coriander leaves and simmer on a medium heat for 5–7 minutes. Garnish with the mint leaves and serve hot with natural low-fat yogurt.

1178 kj; 281 kcals; 15g protein; 7g fat; 0.5g sat fat; 41g carbohydrates; 8.2g sugar; 7.6g fibre; 334mg sodium

masaledaar tofu bhurji (spicy scrambled tofu)

Tofu is an excellent alternative to paneer – as it is lower in fat and higher in protein – and an ingredient that I think is seriously underused in our homes. This dish is quick and easy to make and goes well with whole-wheat roti or granary bread.

1 1/2 teaspoons olive oil
1 teaspoon cumin seeds
2 medium-size onions, chopped
2.5cm piece root ginger, chopped
2 green chillies, chopped
1/2 teaspoon ground turmeric
1 teaspoon ground cumin
1 tablespoon ground coriander
1 teaspoon red chilli powder
2 medium-size tomatoes, chopped
300g tofu, crumbled
2 medium-size green peppers, seeded and chopped
1 teaspoon salt
15g fresh coriander leaves, chopped

1 Heat the oil in a non-stick pan. Add the cumin seeds and sauté until they start to change colour. Add the chopped onions, ginger and chillies, and stir-fry until the onions become translucent.

2 Dissolve the ground turmeric, cumin, coriander and chilli powder in 100ml water and add this to the pan. Cook on a medium heat for 30 seconds, stirring continuously.

3 Add the tomatoes and cook on a high heat for 2 minutes, stirring all the time. Stir in the crumbled tofu, peppers and salt. Mix well.

4 Reduce the heat and cook for 2–3 minutes, tossing frequently to prevent the tofu from sticking. Sprinkle on the coriander leaves and serve hot.

750 kj; 179 kcals; 13g protein; 9g fat; 1.1g sat fat; 13g carbohydrates; 8.1g sugar; 2.8g fibre; 524mg sodium

tofu tamatar ka khut
(sour tofu and tomato curry)

This is a Hyderabadi speciality that is made traditionally with paneer. I have used tofu to reduce the fat content. The texture of the curry is as smooth as silk and this masks the strong sour tang. Enjoy with some brown rice and a salad.

200g tofu
30g seedless tamarind
8–10 medium-size tomatoes, roughly chopped
5cm piece root ginger, roughly chopped
10–12 garlic cloves, crushed
6–8 dried red chillies, broken
1 tablespoon olive oil
1 teaspoon black mustard seeds
1 teaspoon cumin seeds
20 curry leaves
7.5cm stick cinnamon
1 teaspoon ground cumin
1 teaspoon ground turmeric
2 teaspoons ground coriander
1/2 teaspoon salt
35g Bengal gram (dalia), lightly roasted and ground
50ml low-fat coconut milk

1 Cut the tofu into thick strips.

2 Soak the tamarind pulp in 100ml warm water for 30 minutes. Remove the pulp, strain and set aside.

3 Heat a pan and add the tomatoes, along with the ginger, garlic and chillies. Add 100ml water and bring to the boil. Reduce the heat, cover, and simmer for 15–20 minutes, or until reduced by half. Remove the pan from the heat and leave to cool.

4 Pass the cooled tomato mixture through a fine-meshed sieve or a soup strainer.

5 Heat the oil in a pan, add the mustard and cumin seeds, and stir-fry briefly until the mustard seeds begin to splutter. Add the curry leaves, cinnamon stick, ground cumin, turmeric and coriander. Stir-fry briefly.

6 Immediately add the strained tomato mixture. Bring to the boil and stir in the tamarind pulp and salt. Add the ground Bengal gram and mix thoroughly.

7 Reduce the heat and stir in the coconut milk and tofu pieces. Simmer for 2–3 minutes and serve hot.

773 kj; 184 kcals; 9g protein; 8g fat; 1.9g sat fat; 19g carbohydrates; 10.9g sugar; 2.4g fibre; 287mg sodium

tofu rassedaar (tofu in yogurt curry)

Tofu and yogurt are amiable partners. This mildly spiced curry is super-quick to make and goes well with hot rotis. If you want, you can decrease the amount of yogurt and end up with a side dish of dry but well-coated tofu.

250g tofu
1 tablespoon olive oil
1 teaspoon cumin seeds
5cm piece root ginger, chopped
2 medium-size tomatoes, puréed
1/2 teaspoon salt
1/2 teaspoon red chilli powder
1 teaspoon ground coriander
1/8 teaspoon ground turmeric
125g natural low-fat yogurt, whisked
1 green chilli, chopped
1/8 teaspoon garam masala powder
2 tablespoons chopped fresh coriander leaves

1 Cut the tofu into large cubes.

2 Heat the oil in a pan and add the cumin seeds. When they begin to change colour, add the chopped ginger, puréed tomatoes and salt and sauté for 2 minutes.

3 Add the chilli powder, coriander and turmeric and cook for 1 minute. Stir in the yogurt and green chilli and cook for 2 minutes.

4 Add the tofu, garam masala and coriander leaves and serve.

444 kj; 106 kcals; 7g protein; 6g fat; 1g sat fat; 5g carbohydrates; 3.7g sugar; 0.8g fibre; 286mg sodium

palak paneer (spinach with paneer)

This is a favourite Punjabi special. What I like most about it is the brilliant emerald colour of the spinach interspersed with the white of the paneer. Palak paneer tastes best without too many spices and herbs. To get the best results, do not overcook the spinach, since this would adversely affect its bright green colour as well as its taste and nutritional value. Enjoy with roti and/or rice.

900g spinach, blanched
2–3 green chillies, chopped
1 teaspoon olive oil
1/2 teaspoon cumin seeds
8–10 garlic cloves, chopped
1/2 teaspoon salt
200g paneer (see chef's tip page 97), diced
1 tablespoon lemon juice
2 tablespoons skimmed milk

1 Blend the spinach and chillies to a fine purée.

2 Heat the oil in a pan, then add the cumin seeds. When they begin to change colour, add the chopped garlic and sauté for 30 seconds. Stir in the spinach purée and salt, and add water if required.

3 Bring to the boil, then add the paneer and mix well. Stir in the lemon juice and, finally, the milk.

854 kj; 204 kcals; 16.2g protein; 13.1g fat; 7g sat fat; 5.6g carbohydrates; 4.5g sugar; 4.9g fibre; 1285mg sodium

paneer jhalfrezi

This tasty and colourful dish can be prepared in just a few minutes. Indeed, it is easy enough for children to put together with just a little supervision, and you can always add less chilli. Serve with rotis.

2 medium-size tomatoes, halved and seeded
2 medium-size green peppers, halved and seeded
1 tablespoon olive oil
1 teaspoon cumin seeds
2 dried red chillies, halved
5cm piece root ginger, cut into thin strips
1–2 green chillies, chopped
2 medium-size onions, thickly sliced
1 teaspoon red chilli powder
1/2 teaspoon ground turmeric
300g paneer (see chef's tip), cut into 5cm fingers
1 teaspoon salt
11/2 tablespoons vinegar
1 teaspoon garam masala powder
15g fresh coriander leaves, chopped

1 Cut the tomatoes and peppers into thick slices. Separate the sliced onions into rings.

2 Heat the oil in a kadai. Add the cumin seeds. When they change colour add the red chillies, ginger strips, green chillies and onions. Sauté for 30 seconds.

3 Stir in the chilli powder and turmeric, then add the peppers. Cook for 2–3 minutes. Add the paneer and toss. Add the salt and vinegar and cook for 2–3 minutes. Stir in the tomato pieces and garam masala. Garnish with the coriander leaves.

Chef's tip: To make paneer, for every 1 litre milk use 1 tablespoon lemon juice or vinegar. These quantities can vary. Bring the milk to the boil. Lower the heat and add the lemon juice or vinegar. Stir once or twice and continue to cook on a low heat. The milk will curdle in 3–4 minutes. Add a few drops more of lemon juice or vinegar only if the milk does not curdle. Stir once and remove from the heat. The whey of a well -curdled milk is light green in colour. Strain through a muslin cloth and tie it up in a bundle to remove excess moisture. Keep this bundle under a heavy weight for 1 hour if you want a neat block of paneer.

1161 kj; 277 kcals; 15.9g protein; 19.5g fat; 10.3g sat fat; 10.1g carbohydrates; 6.9g sugar; 2.2g fibre; 1598mg sodium

fish and meat

These tempting main dishes can be eaten with vegetables, salad, and rice or roti to make them into a balanced meal. It is important to include vegetables as they supply the nutrients that might be missing from a main fish or meat dish.

Some of these dishes may have quite a high fat content, so make sure you serve with low-fat side dishes.

Recommendations for healthy eating tend to suggest smaller portion sizes for meat than we have given. However, this book is about making realistic changes to your current eating habits, so start with these portion sizes and then, later, if you can cut down some more, you will be doing even better.

tisryanche kalvan
(clams in coconut gravy)

This dish perhaps epitomises the joy of Konkan cuisine. The flavouring from each ingredient is very subtle, but the depth of the blend is what clicks with seafood-lovers like me. As this recipe uses more oil than is usual, please be careful with the fat content of accompanying dishes. Serve with steamed brown rice or whole-wheat rotis, some dal and vegetables.

400g clams (tisrai)
1/2 teaspoon salt
1/2 tablespoon lemon juice
1 tablespoon olive oil
2 medium-size onions, chopped
1 tablespoon minced ginger
1 tablespoon minced garlic
1/4 teaspoon ground turmeric
2 tablespoons low-fat coconut milk
1/2 tablespoon tamarind pulp
2 tablespoons chopped fresh coriander leaves

For the masala
2 medium-size onions, thinly sliced
1 tablespoon olive oil
5–6 cloves
7–8 black peppercorns
5cm stick cinnamon
1/2 teaspoon black cumin seeds
1 teaspoon coriander seeds
3 dried red chillies
2 tablespoons grated dried coconut

1 Clean and wash the clams. Sprinkle on the salt and lemon juice, then set aside for 15 minutes.

2 For the masala, sauté the sliced onions in the oil until golden brown. One by one, dry roast the cloves, peppercorns, cinnamon, cumin and coriander seeds, dried chillies and coconut, then mix with the browned onions and grind to a very fine paste, adding 50ml water.

3 For the coconut gravy, heat the oil in a pan. Add the chopped onions and sauté until light golden brown. Add the minced ginger and garlic and sauté for a few seconds. Stir in the ground masala and sauté on a low heat for 2–3 minutes. Add 300ml water and bring to the boil.

4 Add the clams, turmeric, coconut milk and tamarind pulp to the pan. Cook, covered, for 5–7 minutes. Garnish with the coriander leaves.

659 kj; 158 kcals; 5g protein; 10g fat; 4.2g sat fat; 12g carbohydrates; 7.5g sugar; 2.4g fibre; 272mg sodium

crab masala

Crabs are fantastic if you have the patience to enjoy every bit of tender flesh. I love this recipe for the generous use of coriander leaves, so set aside some time to prepare it and enjoy the irresistible taste of coastal India. This recipe is high in fat so be careful not to have any other fat in your accompanying dishes. Serve with steamed brown rice or whole-wheat rotis and salad.

2 teaspoons olive oil
2 bay leaves
3–4 black peppercorns
2 cloves
2 green cardamom pods
4–5 medium-size onions, finely chopped
1/2 teaspoon ground turmeric
1/2 teaspoon red chilli powder
6 medium crabs (approx. 1kg), prepared by the fishmonger

For the green masala
3 tablespoons chopped fresh coriander leaves
4–5 green chillies
5cm piece root ginger, roughly chopped
10–12 garlic cloves, grated
2 cloves
6 black peppercorns
1cm stick cinnamon

For coconut masala
2 teaspoons olive oil
1 tablespoon coriander seeds
2 black peppercorns
2 cloves
1cm stick cinnamon
3 medium-size onions, sliced
2 tablespoons grated fresh coconut

1 Grind all the ingredients for the green masala into a fine paste, adding about 1 tablespoon water.

2 For the coconut masala, heat the oil in a pan. Add the coriander seeds, peppercorns, cloves and cinnamon and sauté for 2 minutes. Stir in the sliced onions and continue to sauté until the onions turn translucent.

3 Add the coconut and continue to sauté on a very low heat until the coconut turns brown, taking care that it does not burn. Cool the mixture and grind to a very fine paste, adding 100ml water.

4 For the crabs, heat the oil in a kadai. Add the bay leaves, peppercorns and cloves and sauté for 2 minutes. Stir in the green masala and sauté until fragrant.

5 Add the chopped onions, sauté until they turn golden brown, then stir in the turmeric and chilli powder. Sauté for a further 2 minutes.

6 Add the prepared crabs to the pan, mixing in 200ml water and the salt. Bring to the boil, then lower the heat and cook the crabs for 8–10 minutes.

7 Stir in the coconut masala and 100ml water and bring to the boil, then immediately remove the pan from the heat and allow to stand, covered, for about 5 minutes. The flavours will gently seep into the crab.

1894 kj; 451 kcals; 52g protein; 20g fat; 3.9g sat fat; 17g carbohydrates; 10.3g sugar; 3.1g fibre; 1065mg sodium

jhinga do piaza
(prawns with baby onions)

Prawns, like all seafood, are fast to cook, and extremely
good to eat. The addition of button onions in this
recipe improves the texture of the final dish. I love
this with hot fluffy rotis. You could serve with a
kachumber salad too (see page 75).

1½ tablespoons olive oil
1 teaspoon cumin seeds
2 large onions, chopped
1 teaspoon minced ginger
1 teaspoon minced garlic
4 green chillies, chopped
¼ teaspoon ground turmeric
½ tablespoon ground coriander
16 button or pearl onions, left whole
2 medium-size tomatoes, quartered
4 tablespoons chopped fresh coriander leaves
16 medium-size prawns, shelled and deveined
3 tablespoons natural low-fat yogurt
1 teaspoon garam masala powder

1 Heat the oil in a pan and add the cumin seeds. When
they begin to change colour, stir in the onions and
sauté until they turn golden.

2 Add the ginger and garlic, sauté for 1 minute, then
stir in the green chillies, turmeric, ground coriander
and salt. Sauté briefly before adding the shallots,
tomatoes and half the coriander leaves. Sauté for
2 minutes.

3 Add 50ml water and cook for a further 2 minutes,
then stir in the prawns. Cook, uncovered, for 3–4
minutes or until the prawns are almost done.

4 Add the yogurt, garam masala and remaining
coriander leaves. Simmer for 3–4 minutes and serve.

917 kj; 218 kcals; 25g protein; 6.7g fat; 1.1g sat fat;
14g carbohydrates; 9.4g sugar; 2.5g fibre; 263mg sodium

kosha mach (bengali river fish)

Fresh river fish cooked in Bengali style...two greats in one bowl. The first time I tried this dish was at a Bengali friend's home in Kolkata a few years ago, and the taste still lingers in my memory. Cook with ease and enjoy at leisure, just as the Bengalis do. Serve with a small amount of brown rice, dal and some vegetables.

1 small fish (approx. 500g), preferably rohu
1 teaspoon salt
2 teaspoons ground turmeric
1¹/₂ tablespoons coriander seeds
1 teaspoon cumin seeds
3 teaspoons mustard oil
2 medium potatoes (200g), unpeeled, diced
¹/₄ teaspoon onion seeds (kalonji)
5 green chillies, slit

1 Cut the fish into 1cm slices and sprinkle with the salt and turmeric.

2 Dry roast the coriander and cumin seeds briefly. Cool and then grind to a fine paste, adding a little water.

3 Heat 2 teaspoons of the mustard oil in a non-stick pan until it just reaches smoking point. Remove, cool and then heat the oil again on a medium heat. Add the fish slices, a few at a time, and fry for a minute on each side. Drain and set aside.

4 Add the diced potatoes to the pan and sauté for 2–3 minutes. Heat the remaining oil in the same pan, add the onion seeds and chillies, and stir-fry briefly.

5 Now add the coriander-cumin paste and cook on a low heat for a minute, sprinkling on a little water to avoid the masala getting scorched.

6 Add 100ml water to the potatoes and simmer for 4–5 minutes, or until the potatoes are completely cooked.

7 Gently slide in the pan-fried fish slices and simmer for 2–3 minutes, or until the fish is cooked.

Chef's tip: In South Asia, mustard oil is generally heated almost to smoking point before it is used for cooking; this reduces the noxious fumes and reduces the strong smell and taste.

680 kj; 161 kcals; 18g protein; 5g fat; 0.7g sat fat; 12g carbohydrates; 0.4g sugar; 0.6g fibre; 597mg sodium

kolambi bhaat (prawn rice)

This fragrant rice dish is special at home as it's an absolute favourite of my wife Alyona. But I share the recipe with great delight... This goes well with greens – bhindi or karele.

190g brown rice
10 medium prawns (approx. 300–350g), shelled
  and deveined
1 teaspoon lemon juice
1 teaspoon salt
30g fresh coriander leaves, chopped
2 tablespoons grated fresh coconut
3 green chillies, chopped
2.5cm piece root ginger, finely chopped
4 garlic cloves, finely chopped
12–15 fresh mint leaves
3/4 tablespoon olive oil
1cm piece cinnamon stick
3 black cardamom pods, split
1 star anise
3 cloves
1 teaspoon cumin seeds
1 large onion, chopped
1½ tablespoons low-fat coconut milk

1 Soak the brown rice in 500ml water for 2 hours. Drain and set aside.

2 Marinate the prawns in the lemon juice and salt.

3 Set aside 1 tablespoon each of the coriander and grated fresh coconut for the garnish. Grind the remaining coriander and coconut with the green chillies, ginger, garlic and mint to a fine paste.

4 Heat the oil in a thick-bottomed handi and add the cinnamon stick, cardamom, star anise, cloves and cumin seeds. Sauté for 1 minute.

5 Add the chopped onion and sauté for 3–4 minutes, or until it turns light golden brown in colour. Add the masala paste and stir-fry for a further 30 seconds.

6 Add the soaked rice and stir gently for 1 minute. Stir in the coconut milk and 1 litre water. Bring to the boil, stirring once or twice, then cook on a medium heat until the water has almost disappeared – about 30–35 minutes.

7 Add the prawns, reduce the heat and cook, covered, until the rice is tender.

8 Remove the pan from the heat and serve garnished with the reserved coriander leaves and grated coconut.

1199 kj; 286 kcals; 18.7g protein; 6.7g fat; 2.8g sat fat; 40.3g carbohydrates; 3.7g sugar; 2.4g fibre; 678mg sodium

meen pollichathu (fish kerala style)

I have tried this recipe with normal onions, but the result is far superior if you use the more traditional button onions (kunjulli). Instead of pomfret you can use very small flat fish. Serve with roti or/and rice, vegetables and a salad.

4 small pomfrets
1/2 teaspoon salt
1 teaspoon ground black pepper
1 teaspoon ground turmeric
2 tablespoons lemon juice
6–8 dried red chillies
2.5cm piece root ginger
8–10 garlic cloves, chopped
7–8 black peppercorns
1 tablespoon olive oil
1/2 teaspoon black mustard seeds
10 curry leaves
10 button onions (kunjulli), sliced
2 green chillies, slit
2 medium-size tomatoes, chopped
2 tablespoons low-fat coconut milk
4 banana leaves

1 Make gashes on both sides of the pomfrets. Mix the salt, black pepper, turmeric and lemon juice in a bowl and use to coat the fish. Set aside for 30 minutes.

2 Grind the dried chillies, ginger, garlic and peppercorns to a fine paste.

3 Heat the oil in a pan. Add the mustard seeds, curry leaves and button onions and sauté for 2–3 minutes. Add the green chillies and masala paste and sauté on a high heat. Stir in the tomatoes and continue to sauté.

4 Add the coconut milk, then remove from the heat and spread out on a plate to cool.

5 Take a banana leaf, spread some masala on it and place one of the pomfrets on top. Spread some more masala over the fish, then fold in the edges of the banana leaf and secure with wooden cocktail sticks. Prepare the other fish in the same way.

6 Heat sufficient water in a steamer. Place the wrapped fish in the steamer and steam for 8–10 minutes.

7 Serve the fish hot, still wrapped in the banana leaves.

668 kj; 159 kcals; 20g protein; 6g fat; 1.5g sat fat; 5g carbohydrates; 2.7g sugar; 1.1g fibre; 358mg sodium

fish in banana leaves

The highlight of a Parsi wedding, this steamed fish recipe won my heart many years ago! There's no need to reiterate how nutritious fish is, but I would say that if you want to cook fish without oil, this is the recipe for you. Here we have used pomfret, but feel free to use whichever fish you like or is available – just ensure that the scales are removed properly. Serve with roti or/and rice, vegetables and a salad.

8 pomfret fillets (approx. 600g)
4 tablespoons lemon juice
60g fresh coriander leaves, chopped
4 green chillies, roughly chopped
60g grated fresh coconut
3 teaspoons cumin seeds
6–8 garlic cloves
1/2 teaspoon salt
3–4 banana leaves

1 Cut the fish fillets into pieces roughly 5cm x 3.5cm. Sprinkle with half the lemon juice and set aside for 30 minutes.

2 Grind the coriander leaves, chillies, coconut, cumin and garlic to a fine paste. Mix in the salt and the remaining lemon juice, then use to coat the fish pieces. Leave to marinate for at least 15 minutes.

3 Cut the banana leaves into four pieces each. Put one marinated fish piece on each piece of banana leaf, along with a little of the marinade, and fold up the leaves.

4 Heat sufficient water in a steamer. Place the wrapped fish in the steamer and steam for 15 minutes.

5 Serve the fish hot, still wrapped in the banana leaves.

870 kj; 207 kcals; 29g protein; 9g fat; 5.3g sat fat;
2g carbohydrates; 1.1g sugar; 1.3g fibre; 397mg sodium

dum murgh (slow-cooked chicken)

The simple flavours in this recipe mingle together so beautifully that it's hard to describe how terrific the result is. The fragrance that fills the kitchen towards the end of cooking is positively heavenly, and is the signal that the dish is ready for the final sprinkling of spices. Serve with whole-wheat rotis and vegetables.

2 medium-size onions, sliced and roasted (without oil)
5cm piece root ginger, chopped
6–8 garlic cloves, chopped
3–4 green chillies, chopped
375g natural low-fat yogurt
1 teaspoon salt
900g chicken, on the bone, skinned and cut into
   8 pieces
2 teaspoons olive oil
2 bay leaves
1 tablespoon ground coriander
1 teaspoon ground cumin
10–12 almonds, soaked and ground
1/4 teaspoon ground cinnamon
1/4 teaspoon ground mace
1/4 teaspoon ground green cardamom
1/2 teaspoon ground black cardamom
100ml skimmed milk

1 Grind the roasted onions to a fine paste. Set aside.

2 Pound the ginger, garlic and green chillies to a fine paste. Combine this with the yogurt and salt, and use the mixture to marinate the chicken pieces for 2 hours, preferably in the fridge.

3 Once the chicken is ready, heat the oil in a degchi or other narrow-mouthed pan. Add the bay leaves and the chicken (with the marinade) and sauté until the yogurty juices come to the boil. Add the ground coriander and cumin, onion paste and ground almonds. Stir well until mixed.

4 Cover the degchi with a tight-fitting lid, or cover with aluminum foil so that the steam does not escape. Alternatively, you can cover the degchi with a lid and then seal with some dough. Simmer for about 15 minutes, or until the chicken is cooked and the dish is emitting a delicious smell.

5 Uncover the degchi and sprinkle on the cinnamon, mace and ground cardamom. Stir in the skimmed milk and serve.

1055 kj; 251 kcals; 31g protein; 8g fat; 1.7g sat fat; 14g carbohydrates; 10.1g sugar; 1.2g fibre; 658mg sodium

tamatar murgh kofta (tomato chicken dumplings)

These are really simple to make but are a tremendous presence on the party table. Just make sure that you mince the chicken very finely – that way the koftas hold together while being cooked. Serve with brown rice or whole-wheat rotis.

4 boneless chicken breasts (450g), skinned
1 green chilli, chopped
2 tablespoons chopped fresh coriander leaves
1 teaspoon salt
5–6 medium-size tomatoes, quartered
1 medium-size onion, sliced
1½ tablespoons minced ginger
1 tablespoon minced garlic
1 teaspoon red chilli powder
2 teaspoons ground coriander
1 teaspoon ground cumin
1 teaspoon olive oil
½ teaspoon black mustard seeds
8–10 curry leaves
2 teaspoons rice flour
½ teaspoon garam masala powder

1 Roughly cut the chicken breasts into small pieces, then mince along with the green chilli, half the coriander leaves and the salt, until smooth and fine.

2 Divide the minced chicken into 10–12 equal portions, shape into balls and refrigerate until required.

3 Pressure-cook the tomatoes for 5–6 minutes, along with the onion, ginger and garlic pastes, the remaining coriander leaves, the chilli powder, ground coriander and cumin and 200ml water. Open the lid once the pressure has reduced, cool the contents to room temperature, then grind to a fine purée.

4 Heat the oil in pan and add the mustard seeds. When they start to crackle, add the curry leaves and stir-fry briefly. Stir in the tomato purée and 200ml water and bring to the boil.

5 Reduce the heat and gently slide in the prepared chicken balls. Cover the pan with a tight-fitting lid and simmer for 15 minutes.

6 Dissolve the rice flour in 50ml water and add to the pan, stirring continuously. Simmer for 5 minutes, then add the garam masala before serving.

810 kj; 192 kcals; 30g protein; 4g fat; 0.6g sat fat; 10g carbohydrates; 4.7g sugar; 1.6g fibre; 590mg sodium

malvani chicken hirwa masala

The notable feature of Malvani food is its punch. Serve with rice or rotis, vegetables and a salad.

1 teaspoon salt
1 tablespoon minced ginger and garlic
900g chicken, on the bone, skinned and cut into 16 pieces
1/2 tablespoon olive oil
1cm stick cinnamon
2 black cardamom pods
2 green cardamom pods
1 bay leaf
2–3 cloves
1/2 teaspoon cumin seeds
3 medium-size onions, chopped
2 tablespoons low-fat coconut milk
1/2 teaspoon garam masala powder
2 tablespoons chopped fresh coriander leaves

For the green (hirwa) masala
1/2 tablespoon olive oil
1 medium-size onion, sliced
4 tablespoons chopped fresh coriander leaves
1 tablespoon grated fresh coconut
1cm piece root ginger, roughly chopped
4 green chillies, roughly chopped

1 Rub the salt and minced ginger and garlic into the chicken pieces and set aside for 30 minutes.

2 For the green masala, heat the oil in a pan and sauté the sliced onion until it is well browned. Leave to cool and then grind to a fine paste with the coriander leaves, coconut, ginger and green chillies.

3 For the chicken, heat the oil in a pan and add the cinnamon, cardamom pods, bay leaf, cloves and cumin seeds. When they crackle, add the chopped onions and cook until soft and translucent.

4 Add the masala paste and sauté on a low heat for 2–3 minutes.

5 Add the chicken pieces and cook for another 2–3 minutes. Pour in 100ml water and cook until the chicken is done.

6 Finally, add the coconut milk and garam masala, and mix well. Garnish with the coriander leaves.

837 kj; 199 kcals; 25g protein; 7g fat; 2.6g sat fat;
10g carbohydrates; 6g sugar; 1.7g fibre; 585mg sodium

goan chilli chicken

Goan food has always been a hot favourite at home, and this dish has a spicy advantage. Serve with brown rice and/or rotis, vegetables and a salad.

1 small onion, roughly chopped
2.5cm piece ginger, roughly chopped
2 garlic cloves, roughly chopped
3 green chillies, chopped
1/2 teaspoon salt
2 teaspoons lemon juice
8 chicken thighs (approx. 125g each), skinned
1/2 teaspoon cumin seeds
1 tablespoon coriander seeds
1 dried red chilli
2 green cardamom pods
2 cloves
1.5cm stick cinnamon
2 teaspoons olive oil
2 tablespoons tomato purée
1/4 teaspoon sugar
2 tablespoons chopped fresh coriander leaves
1/2 tablespoon vinegar

1 Make a paste of the onion, ginger, garlic and two of the green chillies. Add the salt and lemon juice, then use the paste to marinate the chicken thighs for 2 hours, preferably in the fridge.

2 Dry roast the cumin and coriander seeds, dried chilli, cardamom pods, cloves and cinnamon, and then grind to a powder.

3 Heat the oil in a pan. Add the marinated chicken pieces with the marinade and cook on a high heat. Once the chicken has cooked a bit, add the masala powder and mix well.

4 Add the tomato purée, cook a little, then stir in the sugar. Cook until the chicken is done. Add the remaining green chilli and coriander leaves. Remove from the heat, stir in the vinegar and serve immediately.

1001 kj; 238 kcals; 39g protein; 7g fat; 2.1g sat fat; 4g carbohydrates; 2.4g sugar; 0.5g fibre; 429mg sodium

dahi methi murgh (yogurt chicken with fresh fenugreek)

Another favourite at home, this recipe is effortless but produces a dish fit for a king – the flavours of the fresh fenugreek (methi) and mild spices permeating wonderfully into the chicken, thanks to the marination in yogurt. It is also a great way to cook without fat. Serve with rice or rotis, vegetables and a salad.

225ml low-fat yogurt, whisked
1 teaspoon salt
900g chicken, on the bone, skinned and cut into
    8 pieces
2 x 5cm pieces root ginger
5 green cardamom pods
1 black cardamom pod
5 cloves
2.5cm stick cinnamon
1 bay leaf
1–2 blades mace
2 large onions, chopped
20 garlic cloves, chopped
3 green chillies, seeded and chopped
1/2 teaspoon ground turmeric
1 teaspoon ground coriander
1 teaspoon red chilli powder
2 medium-size tomatoes, chopped
40g fresh fenugreek leaves, chopped
1 tablespoon dried fenugreek leaves (kasoori methi),
    crushed
15g fresh coriander leaves, chopped

1 Mix together the whisked yogurt and salt in a large bowl. Add the chicken and let it marinate for about 30 minutes. Finely chop half the ginger and cut the rest into juliennes. Set aside.

2 Heat a non-stick pan. Add the green and black cardamom, cloves, cinnamon, bay leaf and mace, and roast over a medium heat until fragrant.

3 Add the chopped onions and cook until they turn golden brown. Stir in the garlic, chillies and finely chopped ginger and cook for 2 minutes.

4 Add the turmeric, ground coriander and chilli powder to the pan, along with 50ml water. Stir and cook for 30 seconds. Add the tomatoes and cook until soft.

5 Add the marinated chicken and fresh fenugreek leaves and mix well. Cover and simmer until the chicken is almost cooked.

6 Sprinkle on the dried fenugreek, ginger strips and fresh coriander. Keep the pan covered for about 5 minutes before serving.

938 kj; 222 kcals; 30g protein; 4g fat; 1.2g sat fat; 18g carbohydrates; 11.5g sugar; 2.4g fibre; 651mg sodium

kozhi vartha kari (chicken in pepper sauce)

I love chicken when it's this finger-licking good. The list of spices is long and can alarm those who like their food bland, but the blend is a South Indian classic. And I think that the touch of peppercorns in the final stage is brilliant! Serve with roti or rice and vegetables.

2 dried red chillies, broken
5cm piece root ginger, chopped
6–8 garlic cloves
1 teaspoon red chilli powder
1 tablespoon lemon juice
1 teaspoon ground turmeric
1 teaspoon salt
900g chicken, on the bone, skinned and cut into
   16 pieces
1 tablespoon olive oil
2 medium-size onions, chopped
12–15 curry leaves
3 medium-size tomatoes, chopped
2 teaspoons ground coriander
1 tablespoon tamarind pulp
1 teaspoon garam masala powder
20–24 black peppercorns, coarsely crushed
2 tablespoons chopped fresh coriander leaves

1 Grind the chillies, ginger and garlic to a fine paste. Add the chilli powder, lemon juice, turmeric and salt, and mix well. Coat the chicken pieces in this paste and marinate for 3 hours, preferably in the fridge.

2 After this time, heat ½ tablespoon of the oil in a non-stick pan and sauté the chicken on a high heat until the meat is dry and a little browned. Remove the chicken and set aside.

3 Add the remaining oil to the pan and sauté the onions until brown. Add the curry leaves, stirring well, followed by the tomatoes and ground coriander. Cook until the oil separates from the masala.

4 Return the chicken to the pan with a little water. Cover and cook until the chicken is done and the masala coats the meat.

5 Dissolve the tamarind pulp in 100ml water and add to the pan. Simmer for 10 minutes, stirring occasionally.

6 Stir in the garam masala and crushed peppercorns and garnish with the coriander leaves.

Chef's tip: This chicken dish also works if the chicken is cut into smaller pieces, and it cooks more quickly, too. You can also use entirely boneless chicken pieces (450g), instead of cutting up a whole chicken.

869 kj; 206 kcals; 25g protein; 6g fat; 1.2g sat fat;
13g carbohydrates; 7.8g sugar; 1.6g fibre; 594mg sodium

chicken biryani

This is the eternal favourite for a special Sunday lunch or a party dish. I have simplified the otherwise elaborate assembling of layers of rice, chicken and condiments in order to make the biryani quick and easy to cook. And what makes the recipe even better is that it uses no oil – but the essence of all the flavours is still strong. Serve with a raita and salad of your choice.

285g brown basmati rice
2 green cardamom pods
1 black cardamom pod
4 cloves
2.5cm stick cinnamon
1 bay leaf
50ml skimmed milk
a few strands of saffron
4 large onions, sliced
450g boneless chicken, skinned and cut into
    2.5cm pieces
375g natural low-fat yogurt
1½ tablespoons minced ginger and garlic
4–5 green chillies, chopped
1 tablespoon ground coriander
1 teaspoon ground turmeric
1 tablespoon red chilli powder
¾ teaspoon garam masala powder
1 teaspoon salt
2 tablespoons chopped fresh coriander leaves
2 tablespoons chopped fresh mint leaves
a few drops of kewra essence (optional)
5cm piece root ginger, cut into thin strips

1 Soak the brown rice in 500ml water for 2 hours. Drain and boil in 800ml water with the green cardamoms, black cardamom, cloves, cinnamon and bay leaf for 30 minutes. Drain and set aside.

2 Warm the milk and use to soak the saffron strands.

3 Heat a non-stick pan, add the onions and roast until they turn brown. Set aside.

4 Poach the chicken for 5–7 minutes.

5 In a bowl, mix the chicken pieces with the yogurt, minced ginger and garlic, chillies, coriander, turmeric, chilli powder, half the garam masala, salt and half the browned onions. Transfer this mixture into a deep pan.

6 Spread the rice on top of the chicken in the deep pan. Sprinkle on the saffron-infused milk, the coriander and mint leaves, kewra essence, ginger strips, plus the remaining garam masala and browned onions.

7 Cover the pan with aluminium foil and place the lid on so that the steam does not escape. Place the pan over a medium heat and cook until the chicken is done. This should take 15–20 minutes.

2209 kj; 525 kcals; 40g protein; 7g fat; 2.1g sat fat;
80g carbohydrates; 18.1g sugar; 5.1g fibre; 832mg sodium

saagwala gosht (lamb with fresh greens)

I prefer to add mustard leaves when they are available because of the novelty of their spicy flavour, but this recipe works well using only spinach, too. This is a deliciously easy recipe but quite high in fat, so don't add any fat to your rotis, rice or salad.

250g spinach, blanched and drained
500g mustard greens (sarson ka saag), blanched
  and drained
3 green chillies
1½ tablespoons olive oil
2 bay leaves
2 green cardamom pods
2 black cardamom pods
2 cloves
2.5cm stick cinnamon
1 teaspoon cumin seeds
3 medium-size onions, thinly sliced
3 garlic cloves, chopped
1 tablespoon minced ginger
1 tablespoon minced garlic
1 teaspoon red chilli powder
450g lean lamb or mutton, cut into 2.5cm cubes
1 teaspoon salt
2.5cm piece root ginger, cut into strips

1 Grind the spinach and mustard greens with the green chillies to make a coarse paste.

2 Heat the oil in a thick-bottomed pan. Add the bay leaves, cardamom pods, cloves, cinnamon and cumin seeds. When the cumin seeds begin to change colour, stir in the onions. Cook until the onions are translucent, then add the chopped garlic and mix well.

3 Stir in the minced ginger and garlic, chilli powder and cubed meat. Cook on a high heat, stirring continuously, for 5 minutes. Add 300ml water and cook over a low heat, covered, until the lamb is almost done – roughly 40–45 minutes.

4 Add the spinach-mustard greens paste and salt and cook until the lamb is fully blended and tender. Garnish with the ginger strips.

1414 kj; 338 kcals; 28g protein; 19g fat; 7.6g sat fat; 14g carbohydrates; 6.3g sugar; 2.5g fibre; 692mg sodium

mutton dhansaak (lamb and lentil stew)

The important point in this recipe is to choose lean meat only. The dals add to the protein content and all the vegetables strive to make this a perfect one-dish meal. This recipe is easily prepared using a pressure cooker. Serve with a salad.

50g split pigeon pea (toovar dal/arhar dal)
45g split red lentils (masoor dal)
2 medium-size onions, sliced
2.5cm piece root ginger, chopped
5–6 garlic cloves, chopped
450g boneless lean lamb or mutton, cubed
10 black peppercorns
2 green chillies, slit and seeded
1/2 teaspoon ground turmeric
1 teaspoon red chilli powder
100g pumpkin, diced
3 medium-size aubergines (brinjal), diced
1 large potato (160g), diced
1 teaspoon salt
75g fresh fenugreek leaves (methi), chopped
50g fresh mint leaves, chopped
2 medium-size tomatoes, chopped
2 tablespoons dhansaak masala
3 tablespoons tamarind pulp
30g fresh coriander leaves, chopped

1 Soak the pigeon peas and lentils in 400ml water for 30 minutes. Drain.

2 Heat a non-stick pan. Add the onions and roast on a low heat for 2–3 minutes. Add the ginger and garlic and stir for 3–4 minutes.

3 Now add the cubed lamb to the pan and continue to cook for 8–10 minutes, until the meat is lightly browned on all sides.

4 Stir in the peppercorns, chillies, turmeric and chilli powder, then add the soaked pigeon peas and lentils. Mix well.

5 Add the diced pumpkin, aubergine and potato to the pan, along with the salt and 600ml water. Bring to the boil and cook for 10 minutes.

6 Stir in the fenugreek and mint leaves, followed by the tomatoes. Cover and cook over a low heat until the mutton is cooked – this may take 30–45 minutes. (If you are using a pressure cooker, cook until you hear six whistles.)

7 Once the lamb is cooked, switch off the heat and remove the meat from the pan. Stir in the dhansaak masala and tamarind pulp.

8 Pour the mixture from the pan into a blender, and blend until smooth. Transfer back into the pan and add the lamb. If necessary, adjust the consistency by adding water. Sprinkle on the fresh coriander and cook for a further 5 minutes.

1765 kj; 418 kcals; 35g protein; 12g fat; 4.5g sat fat; 45g carbohydrates; 16.7g sugar; 7.4g fibre; 630mg sodium

keema hara dhania (minced lamb with fresh coriander)

This is a much lighter version of keema masala, and a must for anyone who loves the flavour of fresh coriander. However, it's still high in fat so make sure you don't eat this too regularly and that you don't eat too much fat in your other meals for the day. Traditionally, dill is used as the flavouring, but I like to use coriander when it is available in abundance.

5cm piece root ginger, chopped
10–12 garlic cloves, chopped
3 green chillies, chopped
25g fresh coriander leaves, chopped
4 eggs
1 tablespoon olive oil
1 teaspoon cumin seeds
3–4 green cardamom pods
2.5cm stick cinnamon
4–6 cloves
3 medium-size onions, chopped
450g lean minced lamb (keema)
1 tablespoon ground coriander
1 teaspoon salt
1 teaspoon garam masala powder
4¬5 black peppercorns, crushed
2 tablespoons lemon juice
1 tablespoon chopped fresh mint leaves

1 Grind the ginger, garlic and green chillies to a paste with half the coriander leaves.

2 Cook the eggs in boiling hot water for 12 minutes. Cool, peel, halve and remove the yolks. Cut the whites into quarters. Set aside.

3 Heat the oil in a thick-bottomed pan and add the cumin seeds, cardamom pods, cinnamon and cloves. Fry for 10 seconds, then add the onions. Cook until the onions turn golden brown. Add the ginger-garlic paste and sauté for 30 seconds.

4 Add the minced lamb and cook on a high heat, stirring continuously, for 10 minutes.

5 Stir in the ground coriander, then add 300ml water and bring to the boil. Reduce the heat, cover and simmer for 30 minutes, stirring occasionally. If the meat is still not cooked after this time, add another 50ml water and cook on a low heat until it is fully cooked.

6 Add the salt, garam masala, crushed peppercorns and lemon juice.

7 Stir in the remaining fresh coriander and the fresh mint and mix well. Garnish with the boiled egg quarters.

1593 kj; 382 kcals; 32g protein; 22.3g fat; 8g sat fat; 11g carbohydrates; 4.6g sugar; 1.3g fibre; 657mg sodium

dals

When you cook a dal, you often feel
that you need to add a lot of salt to bring
out the flavour. Don't! Try and use fresh
and dried herbs and spices and lemon
juice to add flavour instead. As a general
guideline, when you are making your own
dals try not to use more than
$1/2$ teaspoon salt per dish for four people.

sookhi moong dal

The secret of making this dry dal is to cook it to perfect tenderness: boil it too much and the dish loses body. Maybe a few first attempts will produce a slightly mashed dal, but go ahead and eat it anyway because the taste is bound to be good. As this uses more than the usual amount of salt, don't eat anything else salty during the day.

250g split green gram, skinless (dhuli moong dal)
1/2 teaspoon salt
1/2 teaspoon ground turmeric
1 tablespoon olive oil
1/2 teaspoon cumin seeds
pinch of asafoetida
5cm piece root ginger, chopped
1 green chilli, chopped
1 teaspoon red chilli powder
2 teaspoons lemon juice
1 tablespoon chopped fresh coriander leaves

1 Soak the dal in 400ml water for 30 minutes, drain, then boil the dal with the salt and turmeric until just cooked but not mashed. Drain off any excess water.

2 Heat the oil in a kadai. Add the cumin seeds and asafoetida. Once the cumin seeds start to change colour, add the ginger and green chilli and sauté for 30 seconds.

3 Mix in the chilli powder, cooked dal and lemon juice. Cook until dry, stirring lightly, taking care not to mash the dal. Garnish with the coriander leaves.

918 kj; 217 kcals; 17g protein; 3.8g fat; 0.5g sat fat; 30g carbohydrates; 1.1g sugar; 5.6g fibre; 267mg sodium

mixed dal

Dals are fun to serve if you can come up with different textures and flavours.

100g split red lentils (masoor dal)
50g split green gram, skinless (dhuli moong dal)
30g split pigeon peas (toovar dal/arhar dal)
25g whole black gram (sabut urad)
pinch of asafoetida
1/2 teaspoon ground turmeric
1 teaspoon salt
2cm piece root ginger, crushed
1/2 teaspoon red chilli powder
3/4 teaspoon ground coriander
1 tablespoon olive oil
1 teaspoon cumin seeds
2 cloves
1 tablespoon chopped fresh mint leaves

1 Soak all the dals in 400ml water for 1 hour. Drain, then mix with the asafoetida, turmeric, salt and 400ml water in a pan. Bring to the boil, reduce the heat and cook until done. Add more water if required.

2 Mash the dal with a ladle and add the ginger, chilli powder, coriander and 400ml hot water. Mix well, then cook for 5 more minutes on a medium heat.

3 Heat the oil in a pan and add the cumin seeds and cloves. When the seeds change colour, add them to the cooked dal and stir well. Garnish with the mint leaves.

822 kj; 194 kcals; 13g protein; 4g fat; 0.4g sat fat; 28g carbohydrates; 1.1g sugar; 3g fibre; 516mg sodium

lauki chana dal (bottle gourd in dal)

This has featured on my weekly menu since I was a child. As this has more than the usual amount of salt, don't eat anything else too salty during the day.

100g split Bengal gram (chana dal)
175g bottle gourd (lauki), skinned and diced
1 teaspoon salt
1/2 teaspoon ground turmeric
1 tablespoon olive oil
1/2 teaspoon cumin seeds
2 green chillies, chopped
pinch of asafoetida
1/2 teaspoon red chilli powder
2 teaspoons ground coriander
2 medium-size tomatoes, chopped
1/2 teaspoon garam masala powder
1/4 teaspoon sugar
2 teaspoons lemon juice
2 tablespoons chopped fresh coriander leaves

1 Soak the chana dal in 300ml water for 1 hour. Drain.

2 Boil the soaked chana dal with the diced bottle gourd, salt, turmeric and 200ml water until done. Mash slightly with the back of a spoon and mix well. Set aside.

3 Heat a non-stick pan and add the oil. Add the cumin seeds and allow them to change colour slightly. Add the tomatoes and cook on a low heat until they soften. Add the green chillies and asafoetida and continue to cook for 1 minute. Add the chilli powder and ground coriander and cook for another minute, until fragrant.

4 Add the chana dal mixture and stir well. Add the garam masala and sugar. Simmer for 2 minutes.

5 Stir in the lemon juice and garnish with the coriander leaves.

520 kj; 123 kcals; 7g protein; 4g fat; 0.4g sat fat;
15g carbohydrates; 2.3g sugar; 0.5g fibre; 516mg sodium

khattu mag (green gram in sour grav

Moong cooked with yogurt has a lovely consistency that goes beautifully with hot bajra or jowar rotis. Gujaratis love this combination with a little sautéed green garlic on the side.

100g whole green gram (sabut moong)
375g natural low-fat yogurt
1/2 teaspoon salt
2 tablespoons gram flour (besan)
1/4 teaspoon ground turmeric
1 teaspoon minced ginger
1 teaspoon minced green chilli
1 teaspoon sugar
1 tablespoon olive oil
pinch of asafoetida
1/2 teaspoon black mustard seeds
1/2 teaspoon cumin seeds
3–4 cloves
2.5cm stick cinnamon
1/4 teaspoon fenugreek seeds (methi dana)
8–10 curry leaves

1 Pressure-cook the sabut moong in 400ml water until you hear four whistles, or until the gram is soft.

2 In a bowl, combine the yogurt, salt, gram flour, turmeric, minced ginger and chilli and whisk well. Add the sugar and 200ml water and mix again.

3 Heat the oil in a pan. Add the asafoetida, mustard and cumin seeds, cloves, cinnamon, fenugreek seeds and curry leaves, and sauté.

4 Stir in the yogurt mixture and cook until the gram flour is cooked. If necessary, add a little water to correct the consistency. Add the sabut moong and cook for 3–4 minutes on a medium heat.

790 kj; 187 kcals; 13g protein; 5g fat; 1g sat fat;
24g carbohydrates; 8.2g sugar; 3.1g fibre; 334mg sodium

gujarati kadhi
(gujarati yogurt curry)

For some time after I got married to Alyona, I used to enjoy this curry as a soup! Now I have learnt the traditional way, served piping hot and mixed with steamed rice.

25g gram flour (besan)
500g natural low-fat yogurt
1 tablespoon grated jaggery
2 green chillies, minced
1/2 teaspoon salt
1 teaspoon olive oil
1/2 teaspoon black mustard seeds
1/2 teaspoon cumin seeds
8–10 curry leaves
2 dried red chillies, broken in half
3–4 cloves
2.5cm stick cinnamon
pinch of asafoetida

1 Whisk together the besan and yogurt until smooth. Add 800ml water, mix well, then stir in the jaggery and green chillies.

2 Cook on a low heat, stirring continuously, until the curry reaches the right runny consistency. Add the salt.

3 Heat the oil in a small pan, then add the mustard and cumin seeds, curry leaves, dried red chillies, cloves, cinnamon and asafoetida. When the seeds begin to crackle, stir them into the kadhi.

476 kj; 112 kcals; 8g protein; 3g fat; 0.9g sat fat; 15g carbohydrates; 11.3g sugar; 0.7g fibre; 347mg sodium (analysis does not include the rice)

relishes, chutneys, pickles and raitas

Spice up any meal and add interest, flavour and even fibre with this collection. Raitas have the added bonus of protein, calcium and often vegetables – they are low in fat and high in taste too.

instant vegetable pickle

This pickle is ready in not much more than 24 hours. It can be stored in the fridge for up to 10 days. This recipe makes 1.7kg. One serving is 1 tablespoon (15g).

500ml vinegar
1³/₄ tablespoons sugar
6–7 black peppercorns
1 bay leaf
15g salt
500g carrots, cut into batons
400g radishes (mooli), cut into batons
250g cauliflower, broken into small florets
1¹/₂ tablespoons mustard oil
¹/₂ teaspoon asafoetida
¹/₂ tablespoon fenugreek seeds (methi dana)
1 tablespoon cumin seeds
1¹/₂ tablespoons split mustard seeds (rai ki dal)
1¹/₂ tablespoons ground turmeric
1¹/₂ tablespoons red chilli powder
2 tablespoons lemon juice

1 Pour the vinegar into a deep pan and heat. Add the sugar, peppercorns, bay leaf and salt. When the mixture is hot, add the carrots, radishes and cauliflower, stir, and then remove from the heat. Keep covered for about 24 hours.

2 The next day, heat the mustard oil to smoking point and cool. Mix the asafoetida into the oil and set aside.

3 Dry roast the fenugreek seeds, cumin seeds and split mustard seeds until they are fragrant. Crush the spices coarsely with a pestle and mortar.

4 Remove the vegetables from the pickling solution and transfer to a bowl. Stir in the crushed spices, followed by the turmeric and chilli powder. Add the lemon juice and mix well. Pour in the mustard oil and mix once more. Keep covered for 4–6 hours and then serve.

33 kj; 8 kcals; 0g protein; 0g fat; 0g sat fat;
1g carbohydrates; 0.8g sugar; 0.1g fibre; 57mg sodium

tamatar chutney (tomato relish)

This chunky, tangy relish goes well with rotis and any rice dish, as well as with grilled fish. This recipe makes 300g. One serving is 1 tablespoon (15g).

3 large tomatoes
4 large mild green chillies
1 tablespoon olive oil
1 medium-size onion, chopped
¹/₂ teaspoon red chilli powder
5–6 black peppercorns, crushed
¹/₂ teaspoon salt
¹/₂ teaspoon ground cumin
¹/₂ teaspoon garam masala powder
2 tablespoons chopped fresh coriander leaves
¹/₂ teaspoon sugar

1 Char the tomatoes and green chillies directly over a flame – you can put them on a skewer for ease. Put them in cold water and then peel. Purée together in a blender.

2 Heat the oil in a pan. Add the onion and sauté until soft. Stir in the puréed tomatoes and chillies and cook on a high heat.

3 Add the chilli powder, crushed peppercorns, salt, cumin and garam masala and sauté briefly. Stir in the coriander leaves and sugar and cook for 4–5 minutes.

4 Serve immediately, or cool and store in the fridge.

51 kj; 12 kcals; 0g protein; 1g fat; 0.1g sat fat;
1g carbohydrates; 1g sugar; 0.3g fibre; 53mg sodium

garlic and mint chutney

This yogurt-based chutney flavoured with burnt garlic and mint is excellent as a dip with baked popadoms. This recipe makes 365g. One serving is 1 tablespoon (15g).

1 teaspoon olive oil
8–10 garlic cloves
1/2 teaspoon black salt (kala namak)
50–60g fresh mint leaves, hand torn
2.5cm piece root ginger, roughly chopped
2 green chillies, roughly chopped
375g natural low-fat yogurt, whisked
1 tablespoon lemon juice

1 Heat the oil in a pan. Add the garlic and sauté briefly. Sprinkle on the black salt and sauté until the garlic is well browned.

2 Grind the mint leaves, ginger, chillies and sautéed garlic to a fine paste, adding two tablespoons water.

3 Stir the paste into the yogurt and mix well. Add the lemon juice and mix again.

4 Pass this mixture through a muslin cloth, squeezing well to get a smooth chutney.

5 Serve chilled.

47 kj; 11 kcals; 1g protein; 0g fat; 0g sat fat;
1g carbohydrates; 1g sugar; 0g fibre; 53mg sodium

roasted pepper chutney

I love this chutney slathered thickly on crisp toasted granary bread. Interestingly, I use cider vinegar in this recipe, but you can use malt vinegar equally well. This recipe makes 285g. One serving is 1 tablespoon (15g).

4 medium-size red peppers
2 medium-size tomatoes, quartered
1/2 teaspoon salt
2 teaspoons olive oil
5–6 garlic cloves, chopped
1 teaspoon red chilli flakes
1 tablespoon cider vinegar

1 Preheat the oven to 180°C/350°F/gas mark 4.

2 Quarter the peppers, and remove the seeds and pith. Place on a baking tray with the quartered tomatoes. Sprinkle on a pinch of salt and all of the oil and roast them in the oven for 20–25 minutes. Peel off the outer skin then chop the flesh.

3 Alternatively, you can roast the peppers and tomatoes directly on a gas flame until the outer skin gets charred. Dip in cold water immediately, then peel off the skin and chop.

4 Heat a pan, add the peppers and tomatoes and cook for 10–12 minutes. Add the remaining salt, mix well, then add the chopped garlic. Cook until the peppers and tomatoes are well blended.

5 Add the red chilli flakes and vinegar, and cook until you have a chutney consistency.

6 Cool and store.

Chef's tip: You can make this chutney using green peppers, too. In which case you could also use green tomatoes instead of red.

57 kj; 14 kcals; 0g protein; 0g fat; 0g sat fat;
2g carbohydrates; 1.9g sugar; 0.5g fibre; 54mg sodium

amla pickle (gooseberry pickle)

The amla, or Indian gooseberry, is an excellent source of Vitamin C. For those who don't want it on its own this pickle can be enjoyed with a meal. This recipe makes 700g. One serving is 1 teaspoon (5g).

15 Indian gooseberries (amla)
120g sea salt
1/2 teaspoon asafoetida
4 teaspoons mustard powder
3 tablespoons red chilli powder
1 teaspoon ground fenugreek seeds (methi dana)
4 tablespoons olive oil

1 Boil the gooseberries with the salt and 400ml water for 20 minutes, or until the fruit is soft.

2 Drain, reserving the brine, then leave the gooseberries to cool. Separate each of the cooled fruit into four segments and discard the seeds.

3 Lightly roast the asafoetida over a medium heat.

4 Mix the mustard and chilli powders, ground fenugreek and roasted asafoetida with 200ml of the reserved brine. Add 6–8 amla segments, then grind to a paste.

5 Mix this paste with the remaining amla segments and transfer to a sterilised jar.

6 Heat the oil until smoking point. Cool, and then pour over the pickle in the jar. Put on the lid and let the pickle stand for about a week before use.

32 kj; 8 kcals; 0g protein; 0g fat; 0g sat fat;
1g carbohydrates; 0.1g sugar; 0.1g fibre; 88mg sodium

chhunda (sweet mango pickle)

Chhunda tastes fantastic just with rotis and parathas. This is a very special sweet-and-sour pickle from Gujarat, made with grated unripe green mangoes. My mother-in-law lovingly presents us with a huge jar of it every year. It keeps well for several months. One serving is 2 teaspoons (10g).

1kg unripe green mangoes
4 tablespoons salt
1 1/2kg sugar
1/2 teaspoon ground turmeric
2–3 tablespoons red chilli powder
2 tablespoons roasted cumin seeds, crushed

1 Wash, wipe dry, peel and grate the mangoes.

2 Heat a deep pan, add the mangoes, salt and sugar and mix. Cook, stirring continuously to avoid the mixture from scorching, until all the sugar melts. Lower the heat and continue to cook, stirring continuously, until a syrup of one-string consistency is formed.

3 Take it off the heat and set aside to cool.

4 Add the ground turmeric and red chilli powder and mix well. Add the crushed roasted cumin seeds and mix.

5 Cool completely and store in airtight, sterilised bottles.

111 kj; 26 kcals; 0g protein; 0g fat; 0g sat fat;
7g carbohydrates; 6.7g sugar; 0.1g fibre; 96mg sodium

palak raita
(spinach raita)

Raitas add that special touch to any meal, whether it's daily food for the family or a feast for guests. This recipe requires very little effort...but the result is gorgeous in all its green glory.

250g spinach
1 green chilli, stem removed
500g natural low-fat yogurt
1/2 teaspoon black salt (kala namak)
1/2 teaspoon ground cumin

1 Blanch half the spinach. Drain, squeezing out any remaining water, then purée together with the chilli. Shred the remaining spinach.

2 Whisk the yogurt and add the spinach purée, black salt and ground cumin. Mix well and chill in the fridge.

3 Heat a non-stick pan. Add the shredded spinach and cook over a high heat for 3–4 minutes, stirring all the time.

4 Continue to cook on a high heat until the spinach is almost dry. Remove from the heat, cool and then chill in the fridge.

5 Combine the chilled yogurt and spinach just before serving.

351 kj; 83 kcals; 8g protein; 2g fat; 0.9g sat fat;
9g carbohydrates; 8.7g sugar; 1.3g fibre; 429mg sodium

lauki raita
(bottle gourd raita)

This is a good way to use bottle gourds. Ensure that you squeeze out any excess water from the cooked bottle gourd.

250g bottle gourd (lauki/doodhi)
pinch of salt
375g natural low-fat yogurt, chilled
pinch of red chilli powder
pinch of roasted cumin powder

1 Peel and grate the bottle gourd. Boil the grated bottle gourd with the salt for 5 minutes. Drain and allow to cool.

2 Whisk the chilled yogurt and add the red chilli powder. Add the bottle gourd and mix well. Serve sprinkled with cumin powder.

248 kj; 59 kcals; 5g protein; 1g fat; 0.6g sat fat;
8g carbohydrates; 5.8g sugar; 0g fibre; 174mg sodium

breads and rice

This section supplies important carbo-hydrates for a balanced meal. Many of the recipes here contain low GI carbohydrates, such as brown basmati rice and whole-grain flours.

Although having carbohydrate through-out the day is essential, too much can make your blood glucose levels rise too quickly, so if you have diabetes, just be aware of how much you are eating in one go...

whole-wheat roti

A basic roti to use every day. This recipe makes eight 13cm rotis.

140g whole-wheat flour (atta) plus extra for dusting
a few drops of olive oil

1 Place the flour in a deep bowl. Add the water in a slow trickle and mix the flour into a sticky dough. Drizzle in a few drops of oil and knead until the dough is smooth. Cover and allow to rest for 15–20 minutes.

2 Divide the dough into eight equal portions and form into balls. Press each ball into some flour and place on a clean surface or board. Using a thick rolling pin, roll out into a flat disc of 13cm diameter.

3 Heat a tawa over a medium heat. Place a roti on the hot tawa and allow to cook for 30 seconds. Flip and cook on the other side for 1 minute.

4 Flip again and press gently with some kitchen paper. The roti will fluff up. Remove from the tawa immediately and serve hot. Repeat for the other seven rotis.

278 kj; 65 kcals; 3g protein; 1g fat; 0.1g sat fat; 13g carbohydrates; 0.4g sugar; 1.8g fibre; 1mg sodium

Chef's Tip: to make chaat masala, dry roast separately 4 tablespoons coriander seeds, 2 teaspoons cumin seeds and 1 teaspoon carom seeds. Let them cool and grind them to a powder with 2–3 whole dried red chillies, 3 tablespoons black salt (kala malak) and ½ teaspoon citric acid. Then mix in 1 teaspoon mango powder (amchur), 1 tablespoon salt and 1 teaspoon ground white/black pepper. Or you can buy chaat masala ready-made from Asian food shops.

masala missi roti (spicy flaky flatbread)

This crisp and mildly spiced flatbread is perfect for spooning up dal or gravy. We can't do without the oil here as it gives the flaky texture that is characteristic of missi roti.

180g gram flour (besan)
105g whole-wheat flour (atta)
60g fresh coriander leaves, chopped
4 green chillies, chopped
1 medium-size onion, chopped
1 teaspoon ground turmeric
½ teaspoon salt
1 teaspoon chaat masala (see chef's tip)
1 tablespoon pomegranate seeds (anardana)
1 tablespoon olive oil, plus extra for greasing

1 Sift together the two flours. Add all the other ingredients, plus enough water to form a soft dough. Knead until the dough is smooth. Rest for 10 minutes.

2 Divide the dough into sixteen equal portions and form into balls.

3 Grease the palms of your hands and also the worktop. Place a dough ball on the worktop and press it down a little to form a disc. Slightly dampen one palm and, using both hands, pat the dough between them to make a roti. Alternatively, you can simply roll the dough on a lightly floured surface, using a rolling pin, until you have a disc roughly 15cm in diameter. Make the rest of the roti in the same way.

4 Heat a tandoor. Lightly dampen one side of each roti and stick it on to the tandoor wall. Alternatively, you can roast the rotis on a hot tawa.

5 Cook until the chapatis are light brown.

285 kj; 67 kcals; 3g protein; 2g fat; 0.1g sat fat; 11g carbohydrates; 0.9g sugar; 1.9g fibre; 68mg sodium

methi thalipeeth (fenugreek flatbread)

The inclusion of bhajnee flour, which is a mixture of cereals and seeds helps to add fibre and lower the GI of this bread. The art of making flatbreads takes a little practice, but why not start now? Serve with a low-fat yogurt. Methi thalipeeth are quite high in calories, so be aware of what else you are eating.

390g bhajnee flour (see chef's tip)
150g fenugreek leaves (methi), chopped
1/2 teaspoon ground turmeric
1 medium-size onion, chopped
1 teaspoon salt
2 teaspoons olive oil, plus extra for greasing
2 tablespoons low-fat natural yogurt

1 In a large bowl, mix the bhajnee flour with the fenugreek leaves, turmeric, onion, salt, olive oil and yogurt. Add water a little at a time and mix to form a soft dough.

2 Divide the dough into eight equal portions. On a moist banana leaf or a thick polythene sheet, flatten each portion into a disc approximately 5mm thick and 10–12cm in diameter. Make a hole in the centre of each one.

3 Heat a non-stick tawa and grease it lightly. Transfer a thalipeeth carefully on to the tawa, and cook on a low heat for 1 minute. Turn and cook on the other side for another minute, or until crisp and golden brown. Cook the remaining flatbreads in the same way.

Chef's tip: to make bhajnee flour, dry roast separately 110g whole-wheat grains, 115g rice, 250g sorghum grains (jawar), 225g millet grains (bajra), 35g black chickpeas (kala chana), 75g split black gram (urad dal), skinned and 25g coriander seeds. Leave to cool, then mix and grind to a fine powder. This will yield 550g flour. It can be stored for up to 1 month.

807 kj; 191 kcals; 8g protein; 3g fat; 0.4g sat fat;
36g carbohydrates; 2.8g sugar; 1.7g fibre; 283mg sodium

ragi dosa (millet pancakes)

This dosa, with its mix of flours, is healthier than ordinary dosas, which are made predominantly of rice. The most unusual ingredient is the ragi (millet), also known as nachni, which provides protein and calcium; it is so easy to digest that it is recommended in India for infants. I have added a few spices so you can eat this dosa on its own. Serve with a chutney of your choice for breakfast or a substantial snack.

300g millet (ragi/nachni) flour
70g rice flour
55g split black gram (dhuli urad dal) flour
2 dried red chillies
1/2 teaspoon coriander seeds
1/2 teaspoon fenugreek seeds (methi dana)
310g natural low-fat yogurt
1/2 teaspoon salt
spray olive oil for greasing

1 Mix the three flours together in a bowl. Grind the chillies, coriander and fenugreek seeds to a paste. Mix the yogurt with 250ml water.

2 Combine the spice paste and flour mixture. Add the salt, followed by the yogurt-water mixture. Mix to a batter of pouring consistency. Let it rest for 3–4 hours.

3 When you are ready to make the dosas, heat a non-stick dosa tawa and spray oil to grease it lightly. Sprinkle on some water and then wipe the tawa clean with a muslin cloth. This is to prepare the tawa as well as grease it lightly.

4 Give the batter a stir, and pour a ladleful on to the tawa, making sure that it spreads in a thin, even layer. Cook until crisp and light brown. Make the rest of the pancakes in the same way.

544 kj; 129 kcals; 5g protein; 1g fat; 0.3g sat fat;
26g carbohydrates; 2.2g sugar; 1.4g fibre; 104mg sodium

jawari bhakri (sorghum flatbread)

There are few breads as simple as this! Cereals such as jawar (sorghum) are high in protein. They are also low in fat and high in fibre. I love eating this bread while it is still hot, all puffed up straight from the tawa.

220g sorghum (jawari) flour

1 Put the jawari flour in a bowl. Add enough water to make a soft dough. Knead until the dough is smooth.

2 Divide the dough into eight equal portions and form each one into a ball.

3 Heat a tawa to medium hot. Meanwhile, take one of the eight dough balls and roll it into a thin round shape.

4 Place the flatbread on the tawa and cook until the underside is light brown. Sprinkle on a little water and then turn the bhakri over to cook the other side.

5 Remove the bhakri and keep warm. Repeat the procedure with the remaining dough.

385 kj; 92 kcals; 3g protein; 1g fat; 0.1g sat fat; 19g carbohydrates; 0.2g sugar; 0.6g fibre; 1mg sodium

hara masala pulao (green pilaf)

This is a delicious rice, with a bit of added flavour to serve with your favourite curry.

285g brown basmati rice
2.5g stick cinnamon
4 cloves
3 green cardamom pods
1 medium-size onion, thinly sliced
1/2 teaspoon salt
800ml vegetable stock

For the paste:
90g fresh coriander leaves, chopped
8 garlic cloves, chopped
5cm piece root ginger, chopped
2 green chillies, chopped

1 Soak the brown rice in 500ml water for 2 hours. Drain and set aside.

2 Make the paste by grinding all the paste ingredients together. Set aside.

3 Heat a non-stick pan. Add the cinnamon, cloves and green cardamoms and, as they begin to change, colour add the onion. Cook until light brown, stirring continuously.

4 Add the drained rice and continue to sauté for 5 minutes.

5 Add the prepared paste and salt. Stir-fry for 3–4 minutes.

6 Add the vegetable stock and bring to the boil. Cook, covered, on a low heat until the rice is done. It can take 35–40 minutes.

1141 kj; 272 kcals; 7g protein; 2g fat; 0.5g sat fat; 59g carbohydrates; 3.5g sugar; 3.7g fibre; 482mg sodium

cauliflower and lemon rice

I have gone a couple of steps beyond the traditional lemon rice (of South India) by adding cauliflower and a rich masala. Enjoy with dal for a fragrant meal.

190g brown basmati rice
1/2 teaspoon salt
pinch of sugar
2 tablespoons lemon juice
4 green chillies, roughly chopped
3 dried red chillies, stemmed and broken
2 tablespoons coriander seeds
5–6 unsalted cashew nuts, roughly chopped
1/4 teaspoon ground turmeric
1 teaspoon olive oil
1/4 teaspoon black mustard seeds
1/2 teaspoon split black gram (dhuli urad dal)
1/8 teaspoon fenugreek seeds (methi dana)
pinch of asafoetida
7–8 curry leaves
500g cauliflower, broken into florets and blanched

1 Soak the rice in 400ml water for 2 hours. Drain the rice, then boil in 1 litre water until just cooked (see the packet instructions), ensuring that each grain is separate. Drain and set aside.

2 Mix the salt and sugar with the lemon juice. Set aside.

3 Grind the green and red chillies, coriander seeds, cashew nuts and turmeric to a fine paste, adding water as required.

4 Heat the oil in a non-stick kadai. Add the mustard seeds, urad dal and fenugreek seeds and sauté until the dal turns light brown. Stir in the asafoetida and curry leaves and sauté for 30 seconds.

5 Add the masala paste and cauliflower and mix well. Add the rice and lemon juice mixture and mix lightly. Cover and cook until everything is heated through.

1020 kj; 243 kcals; 10g protein; 5g fat; 0.5g sat fat;
42g carbohydrates; 3.7g sugar; 3.8g fibre; 346mg sodium

kesari narangi pulao (orange and saffron pilaf)

This subtly flavoured rice is a great one for parties, adding that degree of decadence with the saffron.

285g brown basmati rice
8 medium oranges
a few saffron strands
1 tablespoon skimmed milk
5cm stick cinnamon
2 cloves
2 green cardamom pods
1/2 teaspoon sea salt
7–8 black peppercorns, coarsely crushed

1 Soak the brown rice in 500ml water for 2 hours. Drain and set aside.

2 Thinly pare the rind from two of the oranges and cut it into thin strips. Boil the orange rind strips in water for 1 minute, drain and set aside.

3 Cut all the oranges in half. Extract the juice from all the oranges and reservce eight of the empty halves for serving.

4 Dissolve the saffron in the milk.

5 Heat a non-stick pan. Add the cinnamon, cloves and green cardamoms and fry for 1 minute. Add the drained rice and sauté for 1 minute.

6 Add the orange juice and 400ml water to the rice. Add the sea salt, crushed black peppercorns and orange rind and stir once.

7 Add the dissolved saffron and stir once. Cover tightly and cook on a medium heat until done: about 35–40 minutes. Serve the rice in the reserved orange halves.

1177 kj; 280 kcals; 6g protein; 2g fat; 0.4g sat fat;
63g carbohydrates; 10.1g sugar; 2.3g fibre; 378mg sodium

sweets

Having diabetes doesn't mean you need
to say goodbye to sugar. Small amounts,
especially when mixed in with other high
fibre ingredients, as part of a balanced
diet are fine. Whenever possible, it is
better to keep your sugar intake low by
substituting sugar with dried fruit or
artificial sweeteners. And the best
dessert of all is some juicy succulent
fresh fruit – yum!

matar ki kheer (green pea dessert)

The title of this dessert may sound off-putting, but it is easy to pass it off as the regular pistachio rice pudding! For some time I made my kids eat this without divulging the inclusion of peas because children and peas don't match. Now, however, they don't care because they have learnt to love it! Spoon it up in stemmed glasses for the special effects...

150g peas, fresh or frozen
750ml skimmed milk, boiled
2 tablespoons sugar
1 teaspoon ground green cardamom
6–8 raisins
6–8 pistachio nuts, sliced

1 Blanch the peas. Cool and grind to a fine paste.

2 Put the pea paste in a thick-bottomed pan. Add the milk slowly in a trickle, whisking continuously, to form a mixture without lumps. Cook on a low heat for 10–15 minutes, or until the milk has reduced by half.

3 Add the sugar, ground cardamom, raisins and pistachios, and cook for 3–4 minutes on a low heat, stirring continuously. Remove from the heat and allow to cool before putting in the fridge. Serve chilled.

586 kj; 138 kcals; 9g protein; 2g fat; 0.6g sat fat; 22g carbohydrates; 18.2g sugar; 1.8g fibre; 84mg sodium

gajar halwa (punjabi carrot halwa)

Gajar halwa or, as we fondly call it in northern India, gajrela, is a must as a winter dessert. The challenge here is to retain the full-bodied sweetness of the carrots and not to mask it with added sweeteners. My addition of dates is an attempt to reduce the amount of sugar and make the dessert healthier. However, this dessert is still high in calories and carbohydrates, so be careful about what you eat during the rest of the day, and save it for special occasions. Serves 6.

1 tablespoon olive oil
750g carrots, grated
60g sugar
600ml skimmed milk
120g dates, stoned and chopped
8–10 cashew nuts, roughly chopped
1/2 teaspoon ground green cardamom
8–10 almonds, blanched and slivered

1 Heat the oil in a kadai. Add the grated carrots and sugar and cook for about 5 minutes. Stir in the milk and continue to cook for 10–12 minutes.

2 Add the dates, cashews and ground cardamom, and mix well. Cook for 10–15 minutes or until almost dry. Garnish with the almond slivers.

878 kj; 207 kcals; 5.5g protein; 4.3g fat; 0.6g sat fat; 39g carbohydrates; 37.9g sugar; 4g fibre; 78mg sodium

sheer kurma (vermicelli dessert)

Mustafa, my barman-in-charge in Benares, used to bring sheer kurma for all of us at the hotel...it is heavenly, creamy, and full of ghee and sugar! In this version I have tried to capture the soul of the dish while reducing the calories by using a sugar substitute, but it is still a special occasion dish.

1¹/2 litres skimmed milk
1 tablespoon olive oil
100g roasted whole-wheat vermicelli
a few saffron strands
2 tablespoons sunflower seeds (chironji)
¹/2 teaspoon ground green cardamom
pinch of grated nutmeg
6 teaspoons sugar substitute
3–4 almonds, blanched and slivered
3–4 pistachio nuts, blanched and slivered

1 Boil the milk until it has reduced in volume by roughly a quarter.

2 Heat the olive oil in a kadai, then add the vermicelli, stirring gently. Stir in the reduced milk.

3 Add the saffron, sunflower seeds, cardamom and nutmeg, and cook for about 5 minutes.

4 Stir in the sugar substitute and nuts, taste for sweetness and serve immediately.

1166 kj; 276 kcals; 18g protein; 8g fat; 1.3g sat fat; 35g carbohydrates; 18.4g sugar; 2.6g fibre; 198mg sodium

pineapple yogurt fool

A really healthy, delicious pudding.

½ medium (300g) pineapple, cut into small pieces
2.5cm stick cinnamon
135g hung natural low-fat yogurt

1 Place the pineapple and cinnamon in a non-stick pan and stew over a low heat for 30 minutes. Set aside to cool.

2 Remove the pineapple pieces from the pan and mix them with the yogurt. Blend together in a mixer. Chill in the fridge and serve chilled.

281 kj; 66 kcals; 4g protein; 1g fat; 0.4g sat fat;
12g carbohydrates; 11.8g sugar; 0.9g fibre; 53mg sodium

saeb aur suji halwa (apple halwa)

A comforting dish for a cold winter's day. But as it is high in carbs and sugar, make sure you don't have it too often! Serves 6.

90g semolina (rawa/suji)
200ml skimmed milk
85g sugar substitute
½ teaspoon ground green cardamom
generous pinch of saffron
3 large (450g) apples, 1 puréed and 2 thinly sliced
5-6 pistachio nuts, blanched and slivered

1 Dry roast the semolina, taking care that it does not get coloured. Set aside.

2 Boil the milk with 200ml water in a deep pan. Add the sugar substitute, ground cardamom and half of the saffron.

3 Slowly add the semolina and cook, stirring, until the mixture becomes semi-dry. Add the puréed apple and cook for 2–3 minutes.

4 Divide into four portions. Pack each portion tightly into a bowl, turn it upside down on to a serving plate and de-mould. Decorate with the apple slices, pistachios and the remaining saffron.

663 kj; 157 kcals; 3.3g protein; 0.9g fat; 0.1g sat fat;
36.2g carbohydrates; 24g sugar; 1.7g fibre; 20mg sodium

snacks

South Asian snacks tend to be fried and so are often high in fat – this means you get a lot of calories in each mouthful. And the trouble with snacks is that you often don't realise how many you've eaten and you will still be able to eat a full meal at the end of it. Eat them only for special occasions and try out our ideas here for lower fat versions.

murmura chiwda (puffed rice snack)

Quick and easy, this is a tasty and nutritious snack, reminiscent of (but much healthier than!) Bombay's famous chaat, bhelpuri.

1 tablespoon olive oil
1/4 teaspoon black mustard seeds
2 green chillies, slit
65g roasted split Bengal gram (chana dal)
50g unsalted peanuts
10–15 curry leaves
1/4 teaspoon ground turmeric
120g puffed rice (murmura), roasted
1/2 teaspoon salt

1 Heat the oil in a kadai. Add the mustard seeds, chillies, chana dal, peanuts and curry leaves, and sauté for 2 minutes.

2 Add the ground turmeric, followed by the puffed rice and salt. Toss well.

3 Cool completely and store in an airtight tin.

1055 kj; 252 kcals; 10g protein; 9g fat; 1.5g sat fat; 35g carbohydrates; 1.4g sugar; 0.9g fibre; 255mg sodium

corn bhel (sweetcorn and vegetable mix)

I love this snack when we have our rainy season. Sweetcorn is popular roasted on the cob and then slathered with lemon juice and red chilli. This is a refined version and it's so good you can have it often!

145g sweetcorn kernels
1 large onion, chopped
1 large tomato, chopped
1 medium-size cucumber, chopped
1 teaspoon chaat masala (see chef's tip, page 136)
3–4 green chillies, chopped
2 tablespoons green chutney
2 tablespoons tamarind chutney
3 tablespoons chopped fresh coriander leaves
1 1/2 teaspoons lemon juice
1/2 teaspoon salt
50g pomegranate pearls

1 Boil the sweetcorn, then drain off any excess water. (Note that this bhel can be made with hot or cold sweetcorn.)

2 In a bowl, mix the sweetcorn, onion, tomato, cucumber, chaat masala, chillies, chutneys and coriander leaves. Add the lemon juice and salt and mix again.

3 Divide into individual servings. Garnish with pomegranate pearls and serve immediately.

377 kj; 89 kcals; 3g protein; 1g fat; 0.1g sat fat; 17g carbohydrates; 9.8g sugar; 2.2g fibre; 372mg sodium

baked samosa

Traditionally samosas are deep-fried. Fried foods become more tempting when taboo, hence this baked version of these tasty little parcels. They are such a delight and great for special occasions. This recipe makes eight samosas. Serve with a chutney of your choice and enjoy without guilt!

For the pastry
140g whole-wheat flour (atta)
1/2 teaspoon carom seeds (ajwain)
1/4 teaspoon salt

For the stuffing
1 teaspoon cumin seeds
2.5cm piece root ginger, chopped
3–4 green chillies, chopped
2 medium-size potatoes, cut into small pieces
1 teaspoon red chilli powder
1 teaspoon mango powder (amchur)
1 teaspoon garam masala powder
1/4 teaspoon salt
75g green peas, blanched
2 tablespoons chopped fresh coriander leaves

1 Mix the ingredients for the pastry. Add 65ml water and knead to a smooth, stiff dough. Let it rest, covered with a damp cloth, for 10–15 minutes.

2 Heat a non-stick pan and lightly roast the cumin seeds. Add the ginger, green chillies and potatoes and stir.

3 Add the red chilli powder, mango powder, garam masala and salt. Stir well.

4 Sprinkle over a little water and cook, covered, for 10–12 minutes. Add the blanched green peas and cook for 5 minutes on a low heat. Add the coriander leaves and mix. Let the mixture cool and divide into eight portions.

5 Preheat the oven to 200° C/400°F/ gas mark 6.

6 Divide the dough into four equal portions and roll them into balls. Then roll them into oval-shaped rotis (15cm length, 12.5cm width across the centre). Cut them in half and dampen the edges with water. Shape each half into a cone and stuff it with the potato-and-peas filling. Seal the edges well.

7 Arrange the samosas on a baking tray and bake in the oven at 180°C for 20–25 minutes, turning them every 5 minutes.

Per samosa
373 kj; 88 kcals; 3.7g protein; 1g fat; 0.2g sat fat;
17.1g carbohydrates; 1g sugar; 2.3g fibre; 135mg sodium

ragi panki (finger millet bread)

Panki is traditionally made with rice flour, but I have reworked the recipe using millet (ragi) and whole-wheat flour. As the bread is steamed, it is low in fat, and there's no salt either!

225g millet flour (ragi/nachni), sifted
70g whole-wheat flour (atta), sifted
4 tablespoons natural low-fat yogurt, whisked
1½ teaspoons minced green chilli
½ teaspoon minced ginger
2 teaspoons cumin seeds, roasted and crushed
2 pinches of bicarbonate of soda
8 banana leaves, cut into 12cm squares
spray oil for greasing

1 Mix the two flours in a bowl, then stir in the yogurt and 450ml water. Add the chilli, ginger and roasted cumin and mix. Adjust the consistency by adding more water, if necessary, then stir in the bicarbonate of soda.

2 Lightly grease the banana leaf pieces.

3 Heat a non-stick tawa, then spray on a little oil.

4 Pour some batter on to a banana leaf square and place on the hot tawa. Cover with another banana leaf (oily side down) and cook. Once the bottom banana leaf shows little brown specks on it, flip the panki and cook the other side. (You can make a half-moon-shaped panki by putting the batter on one side of the leaf and folding the other side over.)

5 Make the other pankis in the same way and serve in the leaves.

1080 kj; 257 kcals; 7g protein; 3g fat; 0.5g sat fat;
53g carbohydrates; 2.6g sugar; 3.6g fibre; 152mg sodium

poha with beansprouts

Reach out for a small portion of this mix of flattened rice (poha) and sprouts when you need a filling snack. Trust me, you will enjoy it.

180g flattened rice (poha)
1½ tablespoons olive oil
¼ teaspoon black mustard seeds
10–15 curry leaves
1 medium-size green pepper, seeded and diced
140g beansprouts, boiled for 4–5 minutes
½ teaspoon salt
2 tablespoons lemon juice
2 tablespoons chopped fresh coriander leaves
30g unsalted peanuts
1 medium-size tomato, seeded and diced

1 Place the poha in a colander and wash under running water until soft. Leave to drain for 10–15 minutes.

2 Heat the oil in a kadai and add the mustard seeds and curry leaves. As the seeds begin to splutter, add the pepper and beansprouts. Sauté for 2 minutes.

3 Add the salt, poha, lemon juice and coriander leaves, and toss well.

4 Stir in the peanuts and diced tomato and continue to cook for a further 2 minutes, tossing continuously.

1120 kj; 266 kcals; 7g protein; 9g fat; 1.4g sat fat;
43g carbohydrates; 2.9g sugar; 2g fibre; 255mg sodium

khaman dhokla (steamed gram flour snack)

This spongy snack emanates from Gujarat but has become popular in other parts of India, too. A favourite at home, dhoklas are easy to make, and are also light on both the palate and stomach.

180g gram flour (besan)
250g natural low-fat yogurt, whisked
1 teaspoon salt
1/2 teaspoon ground turmeric
1 teaspoon minced green chilli and ginger
1 tablespoon lemon juice
1 teaspoon bicarbonate of soda
2 teaspoons olive oil, plus spray oil for greasing the thali
1 teaspoon black mustard seeds
2 tablespoons chopped fresh coriander leaves
1 teaspoon grated fresh coconut

1 Sift the gram flour into a bowl. Add the yogurt and around 200ml warm water. Mix well, making sure there are no lumps. Add the salt and mix again. Leave the mixture to ferment for 3–4 hours.

2 Once the gram flour batter has fermented, mix in the turmeric and minced chilli and ginger.

3 Heat a steamer and grease a thali.

4 In a small bowl, mix together the lemon juice, bicarbonate of soda and 1 teaspoon of the olive oil. Add this to the batter and whisk briskly.

5 Pour the batter into the greased thali and place it in the steamer. Cover with the lid and steam for 10 minutes.

6 Remove from the steamer and allow to cool a little, then cut the steamed gram flour into squares and keep warm in a serving bowl or on a plate.

7 Heat the remaining olive oil in a small frying pan. Add the mustard seeds and fry until they begin to pop. Pour over the dhoklas. Serve garnished with the coriander leaves and grated coconut.

886 kj; 210 kcals; 12.4g protein; 6.6g fat; 1g sat fat; 27g carbohydrates; 5.2g sugar; 4.9g fibre; 900mg sodium

spicy tamarind rasam

A rasam is more generally served as an accompaniment to rice in the southern parts of India, but here I present it as a soup. A garnish of roasted garlic can add a great finishing touch. It is possible to buy rasam powder if you don't want to make your own. This soup can charge up the taste buds, can help clear a blocked nose and soothe the throat of many a garlic-lover, it can be a snack...all in all, my aim is to have you try it out!

1 teaspoon olive oil
15–20 garlic cloves
2 tablespoons split pigeon peas (toovar
   dal/arhar dal), soaked
1 medium-size tomato, diced
2 teaspoons tamarind pulp
1/4 teaspoon salt
pinch of asafoetida
1/4 teaspoon ground turmeric

For the rasam powder
1 teaspoon cumin seeds
6–8 black peppercorns
4 dried red chillies
1 tablespoon coriander seeds
1 teaspoon split Bengal gram (chana dal)

For the tempering
2 teaspoons olive oil
1/2 teaspoon black mustard seeds
2 dried red chillies
1 sprig curry leaves

1 Heat the oil in a non-stick pan. Sauté the garlic cloves for a minute, then remove and set aside.

2 Boil 600ml water in a deep pan. Add the pigeon peas and diced tomato and cook, covered, until soft. Mash and reserve.

3 To make the rasam powder, dry roast the cumin seeds, peppercorns, chillies, coriander seeds and chana dal in a non-stick pan until lightly browned. Cool and grind to a powder.

4 Put 600ml water in a pan with the tamarind pulp, along with the salt, asafoetida, turmeric and rasam powder. Bring to the boil and simmer for 5 minutes, or until the raw tamarind smell disappears.

5 Add the mashed dal to the pan and bring back to the boil. Reduce the heat and simmer for 5 minutes. Strain and return to the boil.

6 For the tempering, heat the oil in a pan, then add the mustard seeds, chillies and curry leaves and sauté until the seeds splutter. Add to the boiling rasam. Cover immediately to trap the flavours and serve piping hot.

Chef's tip: You can pound the garlic cloves very lightly before adding to give a better and stronger flavour. You can also pressure-cook the garlic separately and then add to the rasam. Increase or decrease the garlic according to your personal preference.

358 kj; 85 kcals; 4g protein; 4g fat; 0.4g sat fat;
10g carbohydrates; 2.6g sugar; 1.3g fibre; 255mg sodium

mixed sprout ussal (curried sprouts)

When crunchy sprouts meet a coconut and spice masala, something wonderful like this Maharashtrian ussal happens! And, what's more, I've managed to make the recipe work without the addition of any oil. Whole pulses like moong (which produce the familiar beansprouts) are easy to sprout at home. Soak them well, drain and tie up in a muslin cloth. Place in a closed container until the roots start coming out.

½ teaspoon black mustard seeds
6–8 curry leaves
2 medium-size onions, chopped
½ teaspoon ground turmeric
½ teaspoon red chilli powder
1 teaspoon goda masala (see chef's tip)
1 teaspoon grated jaggery
½ teaspoon salt
130g mixed sprouts (e.g. moong, matki, chana)
2 tablespoons chopped fresh coriander leaves
1 tablespoon grated fresh coconut

For the paste
6–7 garlic cloves
3–4 green chillies, chopped
1 teaspoon cumin seeds, roasted
30g grated fresh coconut

1 First, grind the garlic, chillies, cumin seeds and grated coconut together to make a smooth paste. Set aside.

2 Heat a non-stick pan, add the mustard seeds and fry until they crackle. Add the curry leaves and onions and roast, stirring continuously, until the onions turn light golden.

3 Mix in the prepared paste and cook on a medium heat for 3–4 minutes.

4 Add the turmeric and red chilli powder, goda masala, jaggery and salt, and stir well.

5 Add the sprouts to the pan, mix well, and then add enough water to cover just the mixture. Bring to the boil and cook on a medium heat, stirring occasionally, until the sprouts are cooked. Garnish with the coriander leaves and coconut.

Chef's tip: Goda masala is a spice mix typical of Maharashtra. To make your own, roast the following ingredients one by one in a non-stick pan: 70g coriander seeds, 2 tablespoons cumin seeds, 25g stone flower (dagad phool), 6 x 5cm sticks cinnamon, 16 green cardamom pods, 25 cloves, ³/₄ teaspoon caraway seeds, 18 black peppercorns, 12 bay leaves, 1 teaspoon cobra's saffron (nagkeshar), 2 blades of mace, 3 tablespoons grated dried coconut (khopra), 1 teaspoon sesame seeds, 3 dried red chillies and 1 teaspoon asafoetida. When they have cooled, grind the spices to a fine powder. Store in an airtight container, but note that this masala does not have a long shelf life. The above quantities make 50g.

361 kj; 86 kcals; 3g protein; 5g fat; 3.2g sat fat; 9g carbohydrates; 5.1g sugar; 2.1g fibre; 260mg sodium

index

conversion charts

Volume

5ml	1 teaspoon
10ml	1 dessert spoon
15ml	1 tablespoon
30ml	1fl oz
50ml	2fl oz
75ml	3fl oz
100ml	$3^{1}/_{2}$fl oz
125ml	4fl oz
150ml	5fl oz ($^{1}/_{4}$ pint)
200ml	7fl oz ($^{1}/_{3}$ pint)
250ml (0.25 litre)	9fl oz
300ml	10fl oz ($^{1}/_{2}$ pint)
350ml	12fl oz
400ml	14fl oz
425ml	15fl oz ($^{3}/_{4}$ pint)
450ml	16fl oz
500ml (0.5 litre)	18fl oz
600ml	1 pint (20fl oz)
700ml	$1^{1}/_{4}$ pints
850ml	$1^{1}/_{2}$ pints
1 litre	$1^{3}/_{4}$ pints
1.2 litres	2 pints
1.5 litres	$2^{1}/_{2}$ pints
1.8 litres	3 pints
2 litres	$3^{1}/_{2}$ pints

Weight

10g	$^{1}/_{2}$oz
20g	$^{3}/_{4}$oz
25g	1oz
50g	2oz
60g	$2^{1}/_{2}$oz
75g	3oz
100g	$3^{1}/_{2}$oz
110g	4oz ($^{1}/_{4}$lb)
150g	5oz
175g	6oz
200g	7oz
225g	8oz ($^{1}/_{2}$lb)
250g ($^{1}/_{4}$kg)	9oz
275g	10oz
350g	12oz ($^{3}/_{4}$lb)
400g	14oz
450g	1lb
500g ($^{1}/_{2}$kg)	18oz
600g	$1^{1}/_{4}$lb
700g	$1^{1}/_{2}$lb
900g	2lb
1kg	$2^{1}/_{4}$lb
1.1kg	$2^{1}/_{2}$lb
1.3kg	3lb
1.5kg	3lb 5oz
1.6kg	$3^{1}/_{2}$lb
1.8kg	4lb
2kg	$4^{1}/_{2}$lb
2.2kg	5lb

Measurements

3mm	$^{1}/_{8}$in
5mm	$^{1}/_{4}$in
1cm	$^{1}/_{2}$in
2cm	$^{3}/_{4}$in
2.5cm	1in
3cm	$1^{1}/_{4}$in
4cm	$1^{1}/_{2}$in
5cm	2in
6cm	$2^{1}/_{2}$in
7.5cm	$2^{3}/_{4}$in
9cm	$3^{1}/_{2}$in
10cm	4in
11.5cm	$4^{1}/_{2}$in
12.5cm	5in
15cm	6in
17cm	$6^{1}/_{2}$in
18cm	7in
20.5cm	8in
23cm	9in
24cm	$9^{1}/_{2}$in
25.5cm	10in
30.5cm	11in

Published in 2008 by
Kyle Cathie Limited
122 Arlington Road
London NW1 7HP
general.enquiries@kyle-cathie.com
www.kylecathie.com

ISBN 978 1 85626 789 2

10 9 8 7 6 5 4 3 2 1

Designer Geoff Hayes
Editor Sophie Allen
Photographer Yuki Sugiura
Food stylist Valerie Berry
Stylist Wei Tang
Production Sha Huxtable

Azmina Govindji & Sanjeev Kapoor are hereby identified as authors of this work in accordance with Section 77 of the Copyright, Designs and Patents Act 1988.

A Cataloguing in Publication record for this title is available from the British Library.

Colour reproduction by Sang Choy

Printed in Slovenia by MKT PRINT

All dishes serve four, unless otherwise stated. The nutritional analysis at the end of each recipe is for one person/portion.